A FUNNY THING HAPPENED TO ME ON THE WAY TO MY FUNERAL

BY MEL CALVERT

"LIFE IS THAT HARDLY NOTICEABLE SLICE OF TIME,
THAT BLINK OF AN EYE,
THAT OCCURS BETWEEN THE CRADLE AND THE CASKET."
—MEL CALVERT

CONTENTS

INTRODUCTION

Mel Calvert is the only person I have ever known who would sit quietly in the car knowing that I am driving forty miles the wrong way (in my own town!) because he wanted to keep on listening to another passenger and me talking about stories from *The Lawrence Welk Show*. My other passenger was another of my clients, Welk's lead trombonist, Bob Havens, who I was supposed to be taking to catch a flight out of Kansas City International. It wasn't until we were almost a quarter of the way to St. Louis when Mel's wife, Sunny, spoke up and asked, "How far *is* the Kansas City airport, Dave?" We made his plane with thirty-four seconds to spare!

Mel has an uncanny ability to look into a joke or humorous item of almost any kind, dissect it, and see just what makes it work. His reputation is well known among show people of note. In 1978, I was given the honor of producing the Artistry in Cinema Awards ceremony at the Beverly Hilton in Beverly Hills. Our MC, the incomparable Mel Tormé, and I were sitting in his living room in Beverly Hills after rehearsal one evening when we discovered that we both knew Mel Calvert. He told of the time Calvert destroyed the loudmouthed, drunken mayor of San Diego. The two, Mel and Mel, were appearing on the same bill at Art's Roaring 20s in El Cajon, when "Hizzoner" stood up in the middle of a number and disrupted the show. At the close of the show, Mel Calvert, who was doing the emceeing in the main room, finished with, "And while we're at it, ladies and gentlemen, let's have a round of applause for the finest mayor money can buy!" Tormé said it brought the house down. He was so impressed with Mel C. and his showmanship that he gave him permission to use his name in any way he wished on his publicity. Mel C. chose the phrase, *"You've gotta see this act!" –Mel Tormé.* Mel T. said he was pleased that Mel C. didn't go overboard with praise of himself! (I sure am glad that Mel Gibson and Mel Ferrer weren't there, or I would never have gotten this story told!)

I booked the Mel Calvert Show, starring "Sunny and Mel," for the first of eight engagements in one of Nashville's most famous night spots, located at the beginning of Nashville's legendary Printers Alley. If you ever meet Mel sometime, ask him to tell the story of the first phone conversation I had with Mickey Kreitner, the owner of the Captain's Table, in getting that booking. I would tell it now, but Mickey's vocabulary probably wouldn't be conducive to a "family joke book." Besides, no one can tell it like Mel.

We once walked into the pro shop at the Maspalomas Golf Club in the Canary Islands to play a round. Mel pointed to a large glass counter full of slightly used golf balls and said, "Look, Dave, golf balls the size of hail!"

I know you will enjoy this book as much as I did. However, I must caution you: never play golf with Mel! Once, right here in Kansas City, the club announcer yelled over the loud-speaker, "Will someone tell that idiot Calvert to get off the women's tee and back onto the men's tee?!"

Mel yelled back, "Will someone tell that idiot announcer that I'm hitting my second shot!"

Enjoy!

Dave Jackson

Jackson Artists Corporation

Kansas City – Nashville – Hollywood

FOREWORD

After several false starts attempting to find a theme for a book of humor, I decided just to set down some stuff that has happened in the latter part of this life-at-the-speed-of-light I have experienced. A whole lot of it is funny and, hopefully, you will find it tickles your funny bone, too. (I wonder in just what part of the body that bone is located.) I'll throw in some of my favorite jokes, witticisms, and pure nonsense that I have heard, and remembered, over the eight decades of my life, so far. As I am writing this, my Uncle John Calvert is in Las Vegas doing a magic lecture. He just recently celebrated his 101st birthday. If I make it that far, it probably won't be until next week! I'll do my best to include as many as possible that I could tell my grandchildren. There are a few that… well, only a few! I keep remembering that Charlie Chaplin fathered his daughter at the age of eighty. But then, Charlie always was a laugh a minute!

What are my qualifications, you may ask? It so happens that I am actually very famous. It's just that there aren't too many people who know about it! Aside from a king here and queen there, a few presidents, and other heads of various countries around the world, my audience has consisted mostly of the common folk. Punters, as they used to be called in Las Vegas, or *turistas* (tourists) in the Spanish-speaking countries.

When I first got the itch to become a comedian, I started haunting comics wherever I could find them. I lost count of the number of times I sat through every one of Arthur Walsh's performances that I could find, wherever he was performing in and around Los Angeles. One of the most gifted comics ever, in my humble opinion, he had a few supporting roles in several movies, the most memorable one being, *They Were Expendable*, the great WWII classic.

Another one who really gave me a boost was Paul Gilbert. At the Anaheim Bowl, in the early sixties, my first wife and I sat through his first show. Catching up with him on his way back to his dressing room, I found the courage to go up to him and introduce myself. "Mr. Gilbert, I would like to become a professional comedian. Where can I get material?" I asked. "Do you have a lot of money?" he asked. "No," I replied. "Then steal! Did you see my first act?" After answering in the affirmative and telling him how much I enjoyed it, he replied, "Thanks. Stick around for the next show. You'll get some more!" This explained a lot about all the digs at Milton Berle I had heard. But it got me started.

I then found a comedy album by someone I had never heard of, and I memorized it almost in its entirety. Bill Carty was, to me, the funniest comedian I had ever heard but had never seen. So I therefore assumed not many others knew him either, and I was on my way. After a rapid rise in the club circuit, I found myself with a nine-week successful gig in Las Vegas's Fremont Hotel under my belt, and next I headed for the Midwest. I pulled into the driveway of a club in Dayton, Ohio, looked up at the marquee, and felt the blood drain from my face. There, in big letters, was: "Appearing Monday, Directly From Las Vegas . . . MEL CALVERT!" That, however, wasn't what caused my stomach to start break dancing long before that dance was ever discovered. For, right above *my* name, in even larger letters, was: "Now Appearing . . . BILL CARTY!"

For the first two nights, I tried to get by without any of his material, and it was obvious to me that I was dying a slow but inexorable death. Then the club manager had a talk with me and asked me where all the talent was that he had heard so much about from so many club operators out West. I told him the whole truth, and he then gave me some of the best advice I ever got during my entire career in show business. "Just be yourself, kid. I can see why you're scared, but you've got a way of getting people to like you...until they hear the lousy material you're trying to sell them. Just do your thing in your own manner." That turned into one of the best stays I ever had, stateside, and not one person ever said, "Aha, you got that from Carty!"

I was blessed, on both sides of my family, by parents, grandparents, aunts, and uncles who loved to laugh, and it thrills me to see the line continuing through my six children, every one of whom is passing it on. I firmly believe that the greater the sense of humor, the higher the IQ. Once in a while, however, I've run across someone with a great sense of humor but dumber than a doorknob. And, there are those poor unfortunates who think they have a good sense of humor but don't know Victor Borge from Victor Schwartz.

As my youngest son, Michael, once said, "To me, a perfect world is one in which a chicken can cross the road without having its motives questioned!"

So, if you don't like this book, you know why you are having such a hard time with your life. The fact that the chicken simply wanted to get to the other side should be enough for anyone! Or, as Henny Youngman might have said (and probably did), "That was no chicken. That was my wife!"

Mel Calvert

"HERE'S YOUR SIGN."
—BILL ENGVALL

CHAPTER ONE

A SALUTE
TO BILL CARTY

*"I'M ALWAYS HAVING TROUBLE WITH MY WIFE OR THE FURNACE.
IF I WATCH ONE, THE OTHER ONE GOES OUT!"*
—BILL CARTY, FROM HIS ALBUM, BILL CARTY BLASTS OFF

Actually, as has often been stated, there is no such thing as a "new" joke. Almost all humor is based on just a few categories, which really aren't important to this "study." Suffice it to say that one could count on one hand most of the different subjects from which jokes are made.

Here's a good example: Two pigeons are flying peacefully along at three thousand feet, when, suddenly, a commercial jet sends them tumbling end over end as it climbs for the stratosphere. When they recover their pigeon-flying attitude, one says to the other, "Wow, that guy sure was in a hurry!" And the other replies, "You'd be in a hurry, too, if you had two rear ends and they were both on fire!"

I laughed at that joke over fifty years ago when I first heard comedian Paul Gilbert tell it with almost the same setup. Yet, to many of you reading this, that will be a new one…for you, at any rate.

Bill Carty would have been a smash hit in Europe. Being a drinker himself, he knew how to relate and told story after story about the friendly drunk.

Following are some samples of Bill's jokes. (And mine, too, by confiscation.)

This guy comes home late from work with a "load on" and hands his wife his pay envelope. She opens it, looks inside, and yells at him, "Where's the rest of the money?"

"I bought a little something for the house!" he yelled back.

"What?" she demanded.

"A round of drinks!"

A panhandler approaches a slightly inebriated guy on a street in Manhattan. "Sir, could you spare a couple of dollars?"

"Sorry, old buddy, but I don't have any change. Come on in the bar here with me, and I'll buy you a couple of drinks."

"Oh, no, sir. Thank you, but I don't drink."

"OK, then, come on in, and I'll buy you some nice cigars!"

"Thanks, again, sir, but I never smoke!"

"Tell ya what: I'm on my way out to the race track. Come with me, and I'll place a few bets for ya."

"Thanks, again, sir, but I don't gamble."

"You're comin' home with me!" says the drunk.

"Why, sir, should I go home with you?"

"I wanna show my wife what happens to a guy who doesn't drink, smoke, or gamble!"

(Better think seriously about this, all you teetotalers!)

A drunk calls his wife one afternoon and says, "Honey, you gotta come get me. I'm too drunk to drive."

"Oh, all right. Where are you?"

"I'm at the corner of 'Walk' and 'Don't Walk'."

A cop walking his beat around midnight finds a drunk crawling around on his hands and knees under a street light. "What are you doin' down there?" asks the cop.

"I'm lookin' for my car keys," the drunk mumbles.

The cop shines his flashlight around and finally says, "I don't see any keys. Are you sure you dropped them here?"

"No," says the drunk, "I dropped 'em way over there, but there's more light here."

———————————

The pitiful wino had scored a half pint of his favorite wine and was overjoyed! As he was leaving the liquor store with the wine stowed safely in his back pocket (it was a cold, wintry day) he slipped on the icy sidewalk and fell flat on his back. Feeling a liquid running down his leg, he exclaimed passionately, "Oh, God, please let it be blood!"

———————————

A drunk calls the police station and yells, "I wanna report that somebody stole the steering wheel outta my car. Not only that. They stole the brake pedal, the gas pedal, and the whole damn dashboard!"

The officer replies, "All right, sir. We'll get a man on it right away."

A few minutes later, the phone rings again, and the drunk on the other end says, "Hey, ole buddy, you can forget that last call. I was in the backseat!"

It's really hard to find a comic today who knows how to do any material that isn't laced throughout with "Olde English" that they think is current. I like a remark that a friend used to make to anyone using foul words: "Do you kiss your mother with that mouth?" Or, "Hey, it's your mouth; you can haul coal in it if you like." My paternal grandmother had it nailed: "Swearing is the sign of a weak mind trying to express itself forcibly." Bill didn't need shock words.

For another example:

Two Salvation Army ladies are taking a shower after an arduous trek through the streets attempting to save souls. One suddenly looks at the other and exclaims, "My goodness, Mabel, just look at the size of your navel!"

"All right," replies Mabel. "Tomorrow, *I'll* beat the drum, and *you* carry the flag!"

Bill and I finally met in Davenport, Iowa. He was following me this time, and we bumped into each other as I was walking out of the hotel to load something into my car. Even though we had never met, we recognized each other instantly. "Hey, Mel," yelled Bill. "How did my act go here?" It had been some two years since the episode in Dayton, and I had been able to add a lot of new material, but I could hardly keep from falling down laughing. You know that type of person who makes people laugh whether it's funny or not? Carty was funny! We spent a very pleasant hour together, and I poured out my story, the truth. His greatness as a person manifested itself, then and there.

"Mel, I have heard nothing but good about you wherever we have crossed paths. How could I be mad at anyone who has flattered me like this? You are a sorry example of a thief. You don't even try to hide it. I love you!"

Very soon after that, I had the privilege of catching Bill in his club, the Satellite Lounge in Fort Lauderdale, Florida. I felt that I was in the presence of greatness.

MEL CALVERT

MEL CALVERT
HARD TO TELL APART, AREN'T THEY!

Oh, before we go to the next chapter, here's a puzzle from my old (and I do mean "old") producer and on-camera announcer, Jolly Tall Fred King. This is just for the smart people (I'm sure this means you) who are reading this. What do the following words all have in common:

1. Banana
2. Dresser
3. Grammar
4. Potato
5. Revive

6. Uneven

7. Assess

I will include the answer buried somewhere in a sentence later on in the book (just to make sure you keep reading.) And, Fred, I know you will have forgotten the answer by now, so you, also, will have to read on to find it. It will surprise you, and you may want to kick yourself, it's so simple. (I didn't get it.)

SUDDENLY, THERE WAS A CANE!

CHAPTER TWO

LAS VEGAS, NEVADA, PART 1

Speaking of Las Vegas . . . (I definitely spoke of Las Vegas in my Foreword, so if you didn't read it, I definitely talked about it. Go back and read it if you don't believe me.)

A businessman was in Vegas to interview for a very high paying national promotion. He was in the first class waiting room at the airport to meet the executive who would be making the final decision on his qualifications. As he sat there nursing his drink, Frank Sinatra and his entourage walked in and, taking seats, engaged in quiet conversation. The businessman finished his drink and walked up to Sinatra's table and blurted out, "Mr. Sinatra, you don't know me but—" Sinatra cuts him off in mid-sentence with, "Yeah, let's just keep it that way, Clyde!"

So, our hero went back to his seat before the muscle could get ahold of him. He sat there nursing another drink, finished it, and went back up to the table. In a rapid-fire way, he said, "Mr. Sinatra, sir, I'm waiting for my boss to walk in that door to tell me whether or not I'm getting the promotion I have worked so hard for, and if you would just say, 'Hi, Fred, how are you?' he would think you know me, and I know I would get the promotion. Please, Mr. Sinatra, I have a big family and—" Sinatra said, "All right, Fred, go on back to your seat. I'll think about it!"

Within just a few minutes, Fred's boss walks in, spots him at the bar, walks over, and takes a seat. "Say, isn't that Frank Sinatra over there by the door?" "It sure is," says Fred. "Shall we go?"

As they are walking past his table, Sinatra looks up and says, amiably, "Hey there, Fred, how's it goin'?" Fred looks at him and says, "Frank, how many times do I have to tell you: stay out of my life!"

———————————

Rodney Dangerfield, the great put-down artist, got his big break, so legend has it, when Sinatra walked into the lounge in Vegas where Rod was working. The quick-witted Dangerfield paused in mid-sentence and said, "Welcome, Frank. Make yourself at home. Hit somebody!"

Did you hear about the guy who arrived in Las Vegas with a hundred-thousand-dollar Mercedes

and went home in a seven-hundred-thousand-dollar Greyhound bus?

On my opening night at the Fremont Hotel & Casino in Las Vegas, I was given the traditional opening night initiation to the Circus Lounge. The stage was circular and divided laterally by the curtain, which never opened. When the new act was to start, instructions were given by the stage manager to the next act on how to push the button that activated the revolving stage, curtain and all. The finishing act waved good-bye while the new act came into view. On my opening night, I was following a driving and very popular group called the Newton Brothers, the featured brother being a nineteen-year-old kid named Wayne.

As they began their closing number, I was nervous, but ready, and had my finger poised on the button. At the musical break with a drum solo (my cue), I pressed the button and began my entrance. I came on waving with my right hand, playing my keyboard with my left to try to be heard over the big sound of the group as they were leaving. I saw, to my great relief, all kinds of welcoming smiles; no, really huge grins on the faces of the bartenders and waitresses at the foot of the stage. Every eye was on me, and no one paid the slightest attention to the departing Newton Brothers. "Wow," I thought, "this couldn't' have been better! What a great beginning!" My agent at the time, Penny Mayo (he was before Jackson Artists), and the hotel director, Ed Torres, were wearing big smiles as they occupied the VIP booth. And, I was excited! All of this occurring within the few seconds it took for the stage to stop when it hit the center. Only, it didn't stop! It kept on turning, and I waved good-bye to more laughs than I ever got during the entire nine weeks of my first Las Vegas engagement.

Wayne Newton, who had pushed the button to keep the stage moving, and I became friends, spending many an hour fiddling around on my keyboard and making up crazy tunes to the built-in rhythms of my Chamberlin Organ. He, of course, went on to "own" Las Vegas, while I, on the other hand, went on to "own" a far more valuable group: six wonderful kids, seventeen awesome grandkids, and eight or nine (actually, it will soon be ten—I'm losing count) great-grandkids! I wouldn't trade with Newton if he threw in Reno!

———————————

I know a fellow who goes to Las Vegas once a year to visit his money.

———————————

I will, however, give credit to Vegas for giving me the opportunity to learn the finer intricacies and inside knowledge of Blackjack. I dropped my entire first paycheck at the blackjack table in the Fremont, so they had free entertainment for that week. But I spent the next eight weeks, right up to my last night, studying the game. On my last night, I got back my first paycheck times two and then some.

Call it luck, if you wish, but, after a year of playing for an hour or so just about every night in the casino at Hotel Tamarindos in the Canary Islands (don't worry, I'll return to the time line), I was finally banned from the blackjack tables. Not the casino, mind you! The manager came up to me one day and said, "Mr. Calvert, we really appreciate your bringing your friends into the casino, but we must ask you not to play any more blackjack. You have an incredible skill, and we must ask you respectfully not to play anymore."

Several months later, there was a change of ownership of the hotel. The new manager approached me one day and said, "Mr. Calvert, I understand that you used to be a frequent visitor to the casino. What happened?" I told him about being "banned," and he laughed and said, "Oh, I am so sorry. You are most welcome to come and play anything you like!"

So, I resumed my winning where I left off. But, since we were only there for a few more months, they didn't bother me again. They would have lost face, which, by the way, is almost as important to the Spanish as it is to the Japanese.

Nevada – the only state in the union where you will see a sign: "Nine to five, there's a bridge out ahead."

Having worked so long as a single, it took a little time to adjust the act to a duo, especially with someone playing a bass guitar that had never played one before. Sunny, my wife and one of the quickest "studies" I have ever known, learned two numbers on the bass and then faked the rest as I kicked bass on the pedals.

She started her musical studies on a Hammond B3 at the tender age of six and, by the time she was nine, was playing for Mass at her church in Mansfield, Ohio. She went on to piano, graduated from Villa Maria High School in Pennsylvania, a private Catholic girl's school, and from there graduated with a degree in music from the all-girl Clarke College (now a coeducational university) in Dubuque, Iowa.

A memory that will follow me to the grave was a visit we made to her college. A department head, Sister Anne, invited us to lunch with the other sisters. For me, who had been raised a Methodist and was, at this time, a know-it-all agnostic (yes, I know that's an oxymoron—but I qualified as a moron for quite a while in my early life, and the addition of "oxy" was not that much of a stretch), this was an eye-opening experience. There we were, Sunny and Mel "on stage" at lunch with a group of black-clad sisters chatting all around us, and Sister Anne.

I liked her immediately: witty, great sense of humor, and a very astute conversationalist—she talked all about us! As lunch was winding down, a sister stood and announced that one of them was celebrating her birthday and proceeded to lead us all in singing "Happy Birthday" to Sister Agnes. When we finished, I asked, "Sister Anne, why is it that nuns have such beautiful singing voices?" She replied with no hesitation in a stage whisper that carried across the entire room, "Oh, it must be our virginal state!" Among the laughter were a few gasps and at least one "Oh, Sister Anne!"

From that point on, she was absolutely A-OK in my eyes.

———————————

I rescued the following story from oblivion in the *Reader's Digest*:

Sophie and Mary were having a neighborly cup of coffee, when the discussion turned to religion. Sophie said, "Mary, you really can't expect people to believe all that nonsense about walking on water, healing, and turning water into wine, now, can you?"

Mary replied, "Well, Sophie, there were many witnesses and all these happenings were written down and attested to and besides, you should talk. What about the story of Moses's parting of the Red Sea?"

Sophie, looking wistful, replied thoughtfully, "Yes, wasn't that something!"

———————————————

CHAPTER THREE

"PILOT TO COPILOT"

SUNNY WITH OUR PIPER CHEROKEE
(RICK PEEKING OUT THE WINDOW)

It was about this time that Sunny and I decided to take our show off the road and into the air. We bought a

Piper Cherokee and had fun getting accustomed to it with flights between Minneapolis and gigs in Iowa, Ohio, Indiana, Wisconsin, etc.

In fact, in Wisconsin, I wanted to prove to Sunny that I could fly faster than she could run. We had an air-to-ground radio with which we could keep in touch while I was in the air and the rare occasion when she remained on the ground. As I was returning to Stevens Point, Wisconsin, from a trip to the Twin Cities, I contacted her to say I was approaching the motel where we were staying and that if she came out, she could wave at me. As I circled the motel at about five hundred feet, she came out and waved while I waggled the wings of our Cherokee. The airport was only a couple of miles away, and I said over the radio, "I'll race you to the airport!" She started sprinting to the van and stopped suddenly, looking up at me with her hands on her hips. I flew off without considering the necessity of entering the pattern and making the correct approach into the wind on the correct runway. When I landed, I found her waiting for me on the tarmac! It's still hard to put one over on her.

Another time, a couple of years later, we had moved up to a Mooney 8F and were on our way to Provo, Utah, to visit my eldest son, Todd. As we departed from what should have been our final fuel stop in Nebraska and started the long, gradual climb to enough altitude to clear the Rockies, we ran smack into a snowstorm and an eighty-knot head-wind. The snow coming at us was enough to lower visibility forward, but we could make out the cars below us on the interstate. They were passing us! With the eighty-knot headwind, we were making about seventy miles per hour ground speed.

As I filed IFR (instrument flight rules), Sunny, who had been suffering flu symptoms and was leaning up against the cold window on her right side of the cabin, was in misery. She had utilized every container in the plane in which to upchuck, including her fur winter hat. As we labored on, I realized that we would not make it on our fuel supply. Totally immersed in keeping the heading and altitude within the rules, I told her that we would have to land for fuel and asked that she please find us an airport since my calls to Air Traffic Control were going unanswered. She had, for some time now on our travels, assumed all the navigation duties, plus taken over the controls from time to time, and was a quick enough study to be able to allow me to grab a quick nap as we traveled under normal conditions.

But, this time, my request to find us an airport was answered with a simple moan of, "I can't!" "You'd better," I replied, "or we'll land on the side of a mountain!" She straightened up, pulled out the Jeppeson Manual, did a cross check on the Omnis, said, "There should be one right below us," and then re-slumped in her seat.

I banked to the right and banked to the left so I could see below (the Mooney is a low-winged plane) and, sure enough, directly below us were the runway lights. We landed, Sunny spent a little R&R in the Ladies Room while I refueled and re-filed by phone, and off we went. We got to Provo OK and spent a great time watching Todd cheerlead for the BYU football team.

Definition of a good landing: Any landing you can walk away from.
Definition of a *perfect* landing: One after which you can use the airplane again!

Our little dogs, Figaro and Fausto, got their air training in our Mooney early on in their lives. When we arrived in Nashville to play the Captain's Table, Figaro (Fausto hadn't found us yet), who hadn't quite figured out that boy doggies are supposed to lift their legs to go to the bathroom, jumped down from the wing to the ground and, with Sunny on the other end of the leash, made a beeline for a small tree. We watched with anticipation to see if this would be it. He sniffed the tree on his left, sniffed it again, turned back around so he could remain in the same spot, turned once more, decided that this tree would do, and, lo and behold, lifted his leg…the one away from the tree!

Pilots, as a group, are among the elite when it comes to a sense of humor, but, then, so are the ones who keep them flying: the mechanics. After every flight, airline pilots fill out a form called a "gripe sheet," which tells mechanics about problems with the aircraft. The mechanics correct the problems, document their repairs on the form, and then pilots review the gripe sheets before the next flight.

Never let it be said that ground crews lack a sense of humor. Here are some legendary maintenance complaints submitted by pilots (marked with a P for problem) and the solutions recorded (marked with an S) by maintenance engineers. These reports, and more, have been making the rounds in hangars all over the world and are attributed to several airlines. Since they are funny, it doesn't really matter whether they are all true or not.

P: Left inside main tire almost needs replacement.

S: Almost replaced left inside main tire.

P: Test flight OK, except auto-land very rough.

S: Auto-land not installed on this aircraft.

P: Something loose in cockpit.

S: Something tightened in cockpit.

P: Dead bugs on windshield.

S: Live bugs on back order.

P: Auto pilot in altitude-hold mode produces a 200-feet-per-minute descent.

S: Cannot reproduce problem on ground.

P: Evidence of leak on right main landing gear.

S: Evidence removed.

P: DME volume unbelievably loud.

S: DME volume set to more believable level.

P: Friction locks cause throttle levers to stick.

S: That's what friction locks are for.

P: IFF inoperative in OFF mode.

S: IFF always inoperative in OFF mode.

P: Suspected crack in windshield.

S: Suspect you're right.

P: Number three engine missing.

S: Engine found on right wing after brief search.

P: Aircraft handles funny.

S: Aircraft warned to straighten up, fly right, and be serious.

P: Target radar hums.

S: Reprogrammed target radar with lyrics.

P: Mouse in cockpit.

S: Cat installed.

And last but not least ...

P: Noise coming from under instrument panel.

Sounds like a midget pounding on

something with a hammer.

S: Took hammer away from midget.

———————————

It was at a relatively early age that I got the bug for flying. I had three uncles who were pilots and was first turned on to aviation by my Uncle Ray Stevenson, who was an aeronautical engineer. My Uncle Bernard Calvert, who will soon be celebrating his ninety-fifth birthday, was a team leader for General Electric (back when they were "Good Guys") who investigated any crashes involving a GE-manufactured jet engine. He also flew a lot with my Uncle John Calvert, who recently celebrated his 101st birthday by doing a lecture at the Magic Castle in Hollywood and is recognized as the last of the great master magicians of the world. Can't wait to see what he's like when he gets older!

———————————

During my stint with the US Army as an airborne paratrooper, it was in the Jump School at Fort Benning, Georgia, that I was introduced to the grim humor of the jumpers. A student sat through the lecture about how the chute opens automatically with a "static line" and, in the event of a malfunction of the main chute, we have a reserve chute strapped onto our chest, and are there any questions?

"Yes, Sergeant. What if the reserve malfunctions?"

"Well, son," replied the veteran soldier, "you will then have approximately seven seconds to learn how to fly!"

A similar story is about the young guy who heard all the answers given above. At the end, the instructor said, "Upon landing on the ground, you will assemble, and a truck will be waiting to take you back to camp."

As the young guy went out the door of the plane, the buckle broke on the static line. "Not to worry," he thought. "That's what this reserve is for. I'll just give a jerk on the D-Handle ..." as it came off in his hand. "OK, now I suppose that darned truck won't be there either!"

I made a total of nineteen take-offs in big planes before I ever made a landing.

Oh, and by the way, I also learned you do not need a parachute to skydive. You only need a parachute if you wish to skydive twice!

———————————————

I believe that I am the only student pilot who has ever landed a plane backward. The J-3 Piper Cub in which I learned could actually maintain altitude at about forty miles per hour, give or take a couple MPH. Once I was approaching for a landing at the grass strip at the King School of Aviation in Columbus, Georgia, with a forty-mile-per-hour wind right on my nose (that had come up unexpectedly), with half power and full flaps (a big mistake—but I got lucky). I slowly crept over the approach end of the field, settled down to the ground very gently, cut the power, and rolled back about six feet. G. Dean Alan King, Jack's brother and partner, watched the whole thing and proceeded angrily to chew me out for having dumped the flaps into a strong headwind. I let him rant for a bit and then said, "Aw, shucks, Dean. That wasn't so great. Anybody could have done it!" He actually laughed.

———————————————

This funny story has been making the rounds for some time about a student pilot whose instructor had suffered a fatal heart attack. The student, a young innocent lad, wasn't really the sharpest tool in the shed. (I heard this as a "blonde" joke, but I have known some blondes in my life who were much too smart and could see right through me.) Anyway, he grabbed the mike, pressed the button, and said, "Hello!"

Now, among the words an air traffic controller expects to hear on an initial transmission, "Hello" is way down the list.

The controller responded, "Aircraft calling ATC, identify yourself, please."

"Uh, my name's Robert?"

After a slight pause he said, "Sir, are you the pilot?"

"No, I think the pilot's dead."

"Now sir, do not panic. We are going to get you down safely if you can do exactly as I say. What is your position?"

"Uh, I'm sitting in the left front seat."

"Robert, what is your altitude?"

"Well, I'm a little over six feet tall, sir."

"OK, Robert," said the controller very slowly, "I want you to repeat after me, 'Our Father, Who art in heaven' . . ."

For another experience that occurred while I was under the tutelage of the King Brothers, you can go to an article I wrote that was published in the February 2012 issue of AOPA's *Pilot Magazine* entitled, "Xs, Fences and Cows" in the Never Again department. If you are not a pilot or a member of the Aircraft Owners and Pilots Association (AOPA), perhaps Robert could help you (I understand he survived). Or, you can find it at www.aopa.org with just a bit of searching.

In the first week of January in 1985, Sunny and I were appearing at Jumer's Castle Lodge in Peoria, Illinois, when I had one of my most thrilling plane rides. The chief pilot for a major corporation (his name shall remain anonymous to protect the innocent) had seen our show the night before, learned that I was a pilot, and invited me to go with him early the next morning for a check ride on the company turbo jet that had just undergone a periodic maintenance.

I was up before dawn, eager for this opportunity to sit for the first time in the right seat of such a powerful plane. When we arrived, I looked at this beauty sitting on the tarmac and couldn't keep the grin off my face. A Mitsubishi MU-2! Wow! When we entered the cockpit after doing the walk-around, he actually put me in the left seat! The pilot's seat! Not the co-pilot's seat. The real, honest to goodness *Pilot's Seat!*

We started the engines. *We* checked the gages as **We** called for clearance. He had already filed IFR since there was an overcast with a 2,800-foot ceiling, and we were going up and through to the sunshine! As he talked me through the takeoff (he did not touch the controls), we shot off the ground and were in the soup in less than two minutes. I was king of the world! Eat your heart out, DiCaprio! Who needs Kate Winslet?! I'm flying a turbo!

Just then, ATC comes in: "Turbo 42, turn right to One Two Zero." "Right to One Two Zero," I replied in my best airline captain's, well-modulated, very calm, and professional voice. I banked right, glued my eye to the compass, determined to roll out precisely on the 120 mark at which time my "co-pilot" said calmly (you jet pilots already know what's coming), "Uhh, let me help you out just a little here, Mel. We're almost inverted." That's upside-down to you who are solidly but sadly anchored to the ground. It seems that one must learn to scan the dials if one wishes to remain intact in a jet. And, one does not "glue one's eye" to a compass, leaving the attitude indicator to feel neglected.

We broke out on top in less time than it took to write that last, rather humiliating paragraph, and, from then on, he didn't have to touch the controls, not even for the approach and final touchdown. A good instructor can take someone who has never flown but who can follow directions and talk him/her through from takeoff to landing without touching the stick. Except in the rare case when he gets someone for a student who thinks he's Leonardo DiCaprio!

THE MITSUBISHI MU-2

I'm not saying there should be capital punishment for
stupidity, but
why don't we just take the safety labels off of everything
vlem solve itself?

It's been a few years since we retired our last Mooney, but
I have no fear that I could climb in, take off, and land it just as
smoothly as ever!

*MEL AND SUNNY DROPPED INTO THE GULICK FARM
TO GIVE THE COUSINS A CHANCE TO HELP WASH THE MOONEY.*

CHAPTER FOUR

LAS VEGAS, NEVADA, PART II

A Night at the Opera, Vegas Style

Sunny & Mel

JACKSON ARTISTS CORPORATION

*DON'T LAUGH.
THAT'S THE WAY WE ALWAYS STAND.*

Sunny and I worked Vegas a couple of times before we left for foreign ports, and enjoyed some great moments. Among them were those at The Showboat and Frontier Hotels. At The Showboat, a waitress was taking a phone call during which someone had obviously asked about the entertainment. I heard her say, "Yeah, they're pretty good. This tall chick with legs up to her a** lopes all over the stage playing a bass while he stands there behind his keyboard letting her do all the work. He's actually pretty funny, and she's darned good!" I thought to myself at the time, "She can say 'a**,' but not 'damn!'"

But it was at the Frontier Hotel that we experienced what can only be described as a Latter Day *Night at the Opera*! An outstanding entertainer named Billy Kay and his group with his gorgeous wife, Pamela, headlined in the lounge, and Sunny and I caught his show on one of our off nights from The Showboat. In the audience was: Cork Proctor, a journeyman Vegas comic; veteran comedian and all-around nice guy, Norm Crosby; plus, a male vocalist whose name escapes me; and Sunny and Mel.

Billy did a shtick, pantomiming a recording that was very funny in itself, but when he went into the audience and stuck the mike in someone else's face, the startled reaction was ever funnier. After a few such takes, he made the mistake of pushing it into my face, and I immediately picked up on the aria and mouthed it with all the facial expressions I could muster. Billy pulled me up out of my chair and onto the floor where we did an impromptu fake duet that brought the house down. Things went totally Marxist (as in "Brothers") from there.

Another popular number of Billy's was his real sing-a-long, where he would get the people to actually join in on the mike. On this particular night (standing room only), sitting in a wheelchair just off stage right was a nice little old lady having a great time, joining in on the singing and laughing it up. During an instrumental from Billy's group, entering stage left came Cork Proctor, who immediately launched into one of his "evangelist" routines, shouting and frothing at the mouth to the hard-driving number from the group. Spotting the little old lady in the wheelchair, he went over to her, placed his palm on her head, and shouted, "Heal! Heal this good woman!" And, as he started to turn away, she *stood up* and walked toward him! Cork fell on the floor, laughing! The show stopper? Almost, but not quite.

Billy Kay's drummer was a hulk of a Samoan type (some said he was Chinese) with a fantastic sense of humor. As the male vocalist I mentioned earlier had decided to get into the act and began a credible rendition of "Yellow Bird," the drummer got up (seems to me his name was Sammy), left his drums, grabbed me, and pulled me off stage into a vacant dining room where we found a large serving cart. He lay on his back on top of it and, after covering him entirely with a sheet, I pushed him on stage. I wasn't looking at him as we entered while "Yellow Bird" was still tweeting, and so I wasn't prepared for the roar of laughter that erupted. Yes, he was still covered like a cadaver, but I hadn't noticed that he had grabbed a ketchup bottle and was holding it in the upright position in a very strategic place under the sheet!

It was during this stay that Sunny and I suddenly agreed that we should make our arrangement permanent. Along with my beautiful eldest daughter, Mara, we sought out a justice of the peace and found another venue for our show.

While I was taking the whole thing seriously, Sunny, in her nervousness, was being funny. While I repeated my vows solemnly, Sunny took on the voice of Molly McGee's "Little Girl." Was it any wonder, with the almost twenty years' difference in our ages (I'm older) that the JP was looking at me rather sternly? Sunny just had to add a cough right in the middle of, "In sickness (cough, cough) and in health," and it was all Mara could do to keep from coming apart at the seams. I, on the other hand, bravely stayed the course!

At the end of the "ceremony," we paid and suddenly noticed that my daughter had disappeared. Ominous thoughts raced through my mind: "She wasn't really OK with this! She's only been putting on a front! Will I ever see her again?" When, suddenly, she jumped out from behind a bush and threw confetti at us that she had quickly made after ripping several pages from a phone book in a nearby booth.

It runs in the family!

CHAPTER FIVE

RENO, NEVADA

From Vegas to Reno is not that big a jump. We found ourselves still working as a duo in a swank club that has long since gone out of business, as discos had become bigger and bigger. We were happy to be there at the same time as my dad, where he was being treated for just about every conceivable form of cancer. He had been given the traditional "six months" to live (no doctor can know that for sure!) and he was in his sixth year of the fight.

What it was is that Dad couldn't pay the bill, so they kept giving him six more months.

My dad had a great sense of humor that was passed on to me in addition to the great abundance I inherited from my mother's side. So, one morning, as Sunny and I were having breakfast with my dad at *Harolds Club*, I told this one:

This doctor reached for his pen to update a patient's chart and, instead, pulled out a rectal thermometer from his shirt pocket. The doctor growled, "Oh, no. Some a**hole's got my pen!"

My poor father! He laughed until the tears were rolling down his cheeks and, no sooner had he gotten control, than the picture came into his mind again, setting him off even more. People around us were laughing at *him* laughing! I actually feared he would have a heart attack. Six months later, Dad finally passed on. I think he just decided to quit kicking the can down the road.

Another of Dad's favorites was the one concerning the crusty, ever-grouchy and stern Lt. Col. who was being transferred and had to endure what was once a requirement for all field grade officers to go through: a complete physical in order to do a change of stations. He had made plenty of enemies in the hospital ward, when an orderly came into the room to be greeted with: "Well, what do *you* want?"

"Gotta take your temperature, sir," replied the orderly.

"All right, then. Get on with it!"

"OK, roll over, sir."

"Roll over?! What for?"

"Gotta do it rectally, sir . . . Doctor's orders."

And so, after the officer angrily rolled over, the orderly made the insertion and, as soon as he left the room, a young nurse walked in and gave an audible gasp.

"What's the matter," growled the officer, "haven't you ever seen anyone getting their temperature taken before?"

"B-but, sir," stuttered the nurse. "With a daisy?!"

CHAPTER SIX

FORE

Mark Twain has been credited with originating the saying, "Golf is a good walk spoiled." While Twain is one of my favorite humorists and writers, the earliest instance of this general saying is actually credited in 1903 to a couple named "The Allens," but they might not even be the originators. It might be more appropriate to label the saying "anonymous." What's more, there is no substantive evidence that Mark Twain ever used this adage at all.

Whether he ever said it or not, it *is* funny. And we need not worry about Mark Twain having enough material for us to enjoy for hours on end.

A man of the cloth, who was dressed appropriately for the golf course, i.e., without his clerical collar, was approaching the first tee, when a young fellow fell into stride with him, introduced himself as "Steve," and asked if he could play along. The priest readily agreed and, not wanting to identify himself quite yet, introduced himself simply as "James."

So Steve asked, in passing, what his newfound partner's handicap was, to which the priest answered, "Oh, I really have never established one, but I usually play in the low nineties, and you?"

"I shoot about the same. How about we play for a buck a hole just to keep us on our toes?"

"Why not?" responded James.

After the first nine, they were dead even, each with a forty-six, so Steve said, "You know, James, I play better under pressure, so why don't we raise the stakes to five bucks a hole?"

The priest thought to himself, "Here's a good chance to teach this young fellow a lesson. I always play poorly on the first nine, and I will surely be able to finish with an eighty-five or eighty-six. I won't take his money, but *then* is when I will reveal my identity and encourage him to be less rash with his money." He said to Steve enthusiastically, "You're on!"

James shot a respectable forty on the back nine, but Steve ran off five straight birdies on the last holes to finish with a seventy-seven.

After paying off the bet, James said to Steve, "Son, my full name is Father James O' Shea, and I think you should come see me very soon for a good confession. And oh, yes. By the way, if you will bring your father and mother along, I will be happy to marry them!"

Pete, who was recently retired, complained to his wife, "As much as I love golf, my eyes are getting so bad that I have a hard time seeing where my ball is going on my drives."

"Well, honey, why don't you take my brother with you? His eyesight is perfect," replied his wife.

"Good grief, woman. Your brother is in his nineties!"

"So what? There's nothing wrong with his eyes."

So, Pete took his brother-in-law along on his next outing. On the first tee, he hit a screamer on his drive, but soon lost sight of it. "Did you see that?" he yelled.

"Sure did!" said his brother-in-law. "It was a beauty!"

"Great! Where did it go?"

"I dunno," he answered. "I can't remember."

———————————

There are very few games where honesty plays such an important role as golf. It is truly amazing how an accountant can make a great living with putting numbers in their proper place, yet can continuously underestimate the strokes he took on the last hole. There has to be something about a golf course that causes people to lose their memory, their ethics, or both.

Take this case, for example: Your partner slices his ball into the woods, and both of you push your way in bravely to find it. After several minutes, you announce that you are going to go putt out and suggest that he take the stroke and play another ball. But just as you reach the green, your partner yells, "I found it; I'm comin' out!" and a ball sails out of the woods, lands on the green, and rolls to within a foot of the cup. Your dilemma: What do you do as you stand there with his ball in your pocket? Tough decision, right?

———————————

My maternal grandfather, Ray G. Smallwood, one-time county treasurer of Marion, Ohio, was an avid golfer. But he was also an umpire in the Ohio Baseball League back in the thirties. He and his golfing buddy, whose name escapes me (perhaps my Harvard-educated brother will remember it; read this and call me to tell me, but for now I'll call him Sparling) were regular once-a-week habitués at the Marion Country Club.

One day, on the third tee, Sparling shouted at the top of his voice, just as my grandpa was on his back swing, "Where'd ya get those shoes, Ray?"

My granddad calmly put his club in the bag and walked on toward his second shot without a word. Grandpa Smallwood was a master at gamesmanship and kept his partner in suspense until the very last hole. Just as Sparling brought his putter back to make an eighteen-inch putt (they played by the rules—no gimmes!), Grandpa shouted out in his best umpire voice, "Thom McAn's!"

The putt went twenty feet past the cup!

A pro had a bad day and was very rude to his substitute caddie, blaming him for his own mistakes. As he teed up on a short par four hole, he said to the caddie, "OK, this will be good for a nice drive and a short putt," and proceeded to top the ball about ten yards off the tee.

"Now," said the caddie, with a straight face, "for a helluva putt!"

———————————

"Sometimes I just feel like jumping in that lake and drowning myself," said the distraught golfer after putting his drive right in the middle of it.

His partner replied, "I don't think you could keep your head down that long!"

———————————

The detectives arrived at a plush home next to the fairway of the country club and, after entering the house, found a woman with a bloody nine iron in her hand, standing over a man on the floor who was obviously bludgeoned to death.

"What happened here, ma'am?" asked one of the cops.

"I just couldn't take his abuse anymore," she cried. "I had to stop it!"

"Well," said the cop, "you certainly stopped him all right. How many times did you hit him?"

"I lost count . . . six, seven, eight times. Oh, I don't know. Just put me down for a six!"

———————————

So, Bill comes quietly in the door around 8:00 p.m. after promising his wife he would be home no later than 6:00. Before she could get started on her tirade, Bill spoke up: "I know, honey, I promised, but you've got to hear what happened. Poor Charlie dropped dead on the twelfth fairway!"

"Oh, no, dear, that's terrible," she said with sincere sympathy.

"I know," said Bill. "You just can't imagine. From then on it was: hit the ball, drag Charlie, hit the ball, drag Charlie . . ."

———————————

"Hey! You almost hit my wife," yelled the man in the twosome approaching the green of the next hole.

"Sorry," yelled back the husband in the duo following them. "Here, have a shot at mine!"

"I have a tip that can take five strokes off anyone's golf

game.

It's called an eraser."

—Arnold Palmer

ARNIE PERSONALLY GAVE SUNNY AND ME A TOUR
OF HIS CITATION-X JET AT THE ST. AUGUSTINE, FLORIDA, AIRPORT
UPON HIS ARRIVAL FOR INDUCTION
INTO THE GOLF HALL OF FAME

CHAPTER SEVEN

DOGGONE IT

"OH, WHAT A PITY TO WASTE YOUTH ON THE YOUNG."
—OLD GERMAN PROVERB

A very wealthy man was getting ready to back his Rolls Royce into a parking space, when a young twerp slid into the space in his Corvette. As he got out of his car, the young man yelled to the old guy, "That's what you can do when you're young!"

The gray-haired old driver didn't hesitate but backed his Rolls smack into the Corvette, pushing it up on the curb and into the brick building. The young punk screamed, "What are you doing?!"

The old man replied calmly, "That's what you can do when you're rich."

A reporter called on Seth, who was celebrating his one hundredth birthday. As he lay back in his hospital bed, he was all smiles and pleased with the attention. The reporter, after a few minutes of small talk, asked the traditional question: "To what do you attribute your long, healthy life?"

"Well," replied Seth, "I have lived a strictly habit-free life. I've never smoked and have never had a drink of alcohol in my entire life. Not once!"

Suddenly, from the room above there was a terrible commotion with a lot of male swearing. The reporter looked up at the ceiling and exclaimed, "Good grief. What was that?!"

Seth shook his head and said, "Oh, that's just Pa. He's drunk again!"

A Shaggy Dog Story

Tradition has it that the "shaggy dog" story originated in England in the days of yore (that's long, long ago).

A knight on his way to do something terribly important was riding his horse into the ground to get to his destination as fast as possible. After being ridden too hard for too long, his horse became lame, and, seeing a small town ahead, the knight headed straight for the stables there.

"I must have a horse!" he cried. "The life of the king depends upon it!"

The stable keeper shook his head. "I have no horses," he said. "They've all been taken in the service of your king."

"You must have something—a pony, a donkey, a mule. Anything at all?" the knight asked.

"Nothing ... unless ... No, I couldn't."

The knight's eyes lit up. "Tell me!"

The stable keeper led the knight into the stable. Inside was a dog, but it was no ordinary dog.

This dog was a giant, almost as large as the horse the knight had been riding. But it was also the filthiest, shaggiest, smelliest, mangiest dog that the knight had ever seen.

Swallowing, the knight said, "I'll take it. Where's the saddle?"

The stable keeper walked over to a saddle near the dog and started gasping for breath, holding the walls to keep himself upright. "I can't do it," he told the knight.

"You must give me that dog!" cried the knight. "Why can't you?"

The stable keeper said, "I just couldn't send a knight out on a dog like this."

A MORE MODERN SHAGGY DOG STORY

A flying traveling salesman had to make a forced landing in the middle of the Mojave Desert and, having no emergency provisions aboard, he set off walking westward toward the setting sun.

He remembered that there was a ranch with a house only a few miles ahead and so wasn't particularly worried. After a long and hot walk, with his tongue parched and his anatomy dragging, he knocked on the front door.

The farmer opened the door, and the traveling salesman asked if he would be so kind as to put him up for the night so that he could get help first thing in the morning.

The farmer replied, "You're more than welcome, my friend, but I need to tell you that I don't have a daughter."

"Oh," said the traveling salesman, "then could you tell me how far it is to the next house?"

Now, students, be sure you understand that it doesn't necessarily have to have a dog in the story but only that it has an ending that is incongruous, whether or not it ends in a bad pun.

BUT IT'S ALWAYS NICE TO HAVE A DOG!

Ready for Another One?

A young man had reached a point in his life when he came to the conclusion that he really didn't know what the meaning of it all was. He vowed to do what it takes, go where he must, regardless of the cost in money and effort to find it.

Selling all his belongings, he had enough to buy a plane fare to Nepal at the foot of the Himalaya Mountains, where there was an old but very wise man who could tell him the meaning of life. The young man was warned by a local Tibetan priest that, in order to prove himself, he must take with him only what water and provisions he could carry to make the trek and tortuous climb up to the summit where the wise one lived. Also he had to make the climb barefooted—no sandals or covering of any kind on his feet.

And so, very early in the morning, he set off with directions given to him by the priest. He walked and walked for miles, with the path becoming narrower and narrower and steeper and steeper, until there was nothing but bare rock, which he had to grasp to pull himself up one agonizing meter at a time. His feet and hands soon became torn and bloody from the sharp rocks over which he was climbing. He had long ago used his last water and food, and his thirst was almost unbearable.

Finally, after what seemed like days but, in fact, was only several hours, he reached the summit and saw a small hut that seemed to be deserted. As he cautiously approached, he heard the humming of a voice from within the hut: "Ommmm, Ommmm." He drew nearer and, suddenly, the humming stopped, and a voice called out, "Come in, my son. I've been expecting you!" He entered and, as his eyes became accustomed, he saw the ancient one wearing only a wraparound white sheet, sitting cross-legged in the center of the small hovel.

"You have come to learn the meaning of life, have you not?" he asked.

"Yes, oh, Wise One," he replied.

Seeing the condition of the young man's feet and hands, the old one said, "You have proved yourself, my son. Please, sit. I shall tell you. But first, wash your hands and face in the basin in front of you, and take a drink from the jug beside it."

His heart racing with anticipation, the young man did as he was told. When he finished, the old one smiled, looked at him warmly and intently, and very slowly, with much reverence in his voice, said, "Life, my son, is a fountain." The old man paused and spoke no more, but continued to stare into the young man's face.

Finally, with a trembling voice, the young man murmured, "Life . . . is a fountain?"

The old man, visibly shaken, with obvious consternation asked, "You mean . . . life is . . . *not* a fountain?"

That shaggy dog story was told to me by one of the most talented jazz pianists I have ever known, Meredith "Mickey" McClain, and will guarantee a great variance of reactions if you will learn to tell it well. It is one of the best shaggy dog stories I have ever heard, and Mickey, who was my piano man for a while before he was stolen from me by Buddy Rich (the insanely talented drummer/leader of the Buddy Rich big band), told it as well as anyone, including me.

Mickey was working with me when I did a two week gig at The Depot, in Rochester, Minnesota, home of the Mayo Clinic. (Minnesota is also the home of the Vikings, Michelle Bachman, ten thousand lakes [and ten thousand fish] and the Minnesota state bird, the mosquito—not necessarily in order of importance.)

A couple of very well-known personalities were in the audience at different times, Danny Kaye and Johnny Carson. I had a running gag going with a handsome young guitarist who strolled and sang to the diners in the restaurant adjacent to the show lounge, which was separated only by a curtain. Sometimes I opened the curtain just enough for Tommy to be able to see me when he looked up, and I then proceeded to make all kinds of faces to crack him up while he was singing. It never failed.

Never, that is, until the night Danny Kaye was dining, spied me, and stopped in midbite to watch the fun. Do you think that Tommy would look up, even once? Oh, no! Not with a celebrity watching! Of course not! He had gotten his revenge!

From the same vantage point, I overheard Carson one night on the phone saying that, for such a hick town as Rochester, the entertainment was above average. I waited in vain for the invitation from his producer.

Paddy, after celebrating his eightieth birthday, was weaving his way home by way of the cemetery, and stumbled into an open grave. Try as he might, he just couldn't pull his way out and decided to go to sleep and wait for the people to come in the morning to pull him out. It was a very dark night, and soon young Bill O'Rourke, with a little more than a snoot full, came along the same path and fell into the same grave. After Bill tried to get out a couple of times, Paddy woke up, watched Bill try once more, and said, his voice coming from the darkest corner of the grave, "You'll never get out!" . . . But he did!

———————————

OK, that wasn't really a shaggy dog story. So following is one more in the Irish manner:

O'Reilly was born with a humpback and, growing up with it, he was accustomed to it as were all his chums at the pub. One night, after a night of partying, he was wending his way home (through the same cemetery, of course!), when a voice came from out of the darkness: "Hello, there!"

O'Reilly cried out nervously, "Who's there?"

"'Tis I, the Angel Gabriel. Where are you going?"

"Well, I was just on me way home from the pub, and I decided to take a shortcut through the cemetery," answered O'Reilly.

"Why do you walk that way?" asked the voice.

"Well, I have a humpback. I've had it since I was a wee lad," replied O'Reilly.

"Well, here, allow me!"

O'Reilly felt a sensation on his back and, suddenly, he could stand up straight, and the hump was gone!

Racing back to the pub and bursting in the door, he exclaimed, "Look at me! Look at me, everyone! My hump is gone!"

"What happened?" called out O'Shaughnessy.

"I was on me way home, takin' a shortcut through the cemetery, and . . ." He continued on, filling them in on the strange event.

So, O'Toole, who had been born with a clubfoot, hobbled quietly out the door and headed for the cemetery. He walked along, nervously whistling loudly, and, sure enough, the voice came from out of the darkness: "Hello there!"

"Is that you, Gabriel?" asked O'Toole in a tight voice.

"Yes, indeed, it is I, Gabriel. Where are you going?"

Remembering O'Reilly's words, he repeated them exactly, "Well, I was just on me way home from the pub, and I decided to take a shortcut through the cemetery."

"Why do you walk that way?" asked Gabriel.

"It's a clubfoot. I've had it since I was a wee lad. *So will ya just get on with it, and do yer thing!*"

"Well, of course. Here, have a humpback to go with it!"

More often than not, it pays to ask nicely!

A highly respected ophthalmologist and a pillar of the community decided the time had come to retire. Several people in town, wishing to show their appreciation for all he had done for people, decided to throw a surprise party for him. His wife got him out of the house on a pretext, and everyone who was anyone congregated in his home. Among them was a commercial illustrator who had painted a portrait of the good doctor, which they hung on his den wall and covered with a velvet drape.

When the doctor and his wife returned, he was properly shocked but pleased, and, after the party had begun to settle down, the time came to take him into his den and unveil the portrait. As everyone gathered around him, the drape was pulled away to reveal the doctor's image cleverly imbedded in the iris of a giant eye.

He was visibly moved and, as the applause died down, a reporter from the local newspaper asked, "Doctor, what was your first thought as you looked at the portrait and realized the love for you that all have shown you today?"

"Well, to tell you the truth, my first thought was, 'Thank God I had not become a proctologist'!" (*You will have to picture this yourself. The editor would not allow me to insert a photo.*)

During their sixtieth wedding anniversary party, the old man pooped out early and went upstairs to bed. Soon his wife came in and said, "Honey, it's our anniversary, and we're having a party!"

"I know it, woman. You're makin' enough noise to wake the dead!" he growled.

"Well, can't you just give me a little kiss on the cheek?" she begged.

"Come on, woman. I have to get up in the morning and walk the dog!"

"Well, couldn't you at least give me a little bite on the ear?" she pleaded.

"Look, woman, my teeth are in the bathroom. Go bite your own damn ear!"

CHAPTER EIGHT

GULLIBLE'S TRAVELS

"CAUSE I'M LEAVIN'

ON A JET PLANE.

DON'T KNOW

WHEN I'LL BE BACK AGAIN."

—PETER, PAUL & MARY (WRITTEN BY JOHN DENVER)

One of the last gigs we had before leaving the states was in Great Falls, Montana. On our way into town, and before we found the club, we were hungry and had a yen for some oriental food (pun intended). I pulled into a station where a young guy was checking his oil and asked him, "Hi, do you have an Oriental restaurant in town?"

He paused, scratched his head, and said, "No, sir, I don't believe… Annie, do we have any Oriental restaurants in Great Falls?"

The lady in his car thought and slowly shook her head. "Not that I know of."

"You mean, you don't have a Chinese restaurant in all of Great Falls?" I asked incredulously.

"Oh, yeah, we've got two *Chinese* restaurants!" he said as they both nodded their heads enthusiastically.

So, even though there were no Oriental eateries, we had a great stay in Great Falls!

A group of airmen and their mates became fans of ours and invited us to a party after our show one night. The fun went on into the wee hours, and I did some close-up magic and "stole" a watch or two. When the time came to leave, one of three guys from the "hood," who had been shooting craps, held up a pair of dice and said with a challenge, "Here, let's see you throw a 'seven'!"

I took the dice and, as a joke, I said, "Why not? At least it will keep me from ever getting dragged into a game with you, won't it?!" Everyone laughed as I casually took the dice and threw . . . a seven!

Among the gasps and *oohs* and *ahs*, the same fellow said, "Let's see you do that again. I want to watch you closer this time!"

Determined to let them know that it was all a joke, I took the dice again. Before throwing them, I said, with much pomp, "OK, just one more time, but I will not tell you how to do it. That just wouldn't be honest, and, besides, it just might get you in real trouble sometime!"

I was waiting for the laughter as I threw the dice again, expecting the odds to kick in, but, so help me, the ghost of Harry Blackstone or Houdini had to have interfered, and out came another seven. With that, Sunny and I said "good night" to a bunch of people who, to this day, I am sure, think they saw someone who knew how to control a pair of dice.

————————————————

Americans who have not traveled a lot have a hard time understanding why everyone doesn't speak English. I should talk! Here's one that happened to me:

When we arrived in the Virgin Islands, which was really our first trip out of continental North America, I was listening to the baggage guys chattering in a language I simply could not recognize. After all, I speak Spanish fluently, and it definitely was not that, nor French, or Portuguese, and certainly not Italian. What could it possibly be?

So I asked John, the supervisor in charge of the unloading, "John, please tell me what language you are speaking. I pride myself on being a linguist, but I don't recognize it at all. Is it some sort of Virgin Island dialect? Please help me out here."

John looked at me and, with a broad smile, said, "It's English, Mon!"

I wasn't listening for English! I'm sure he was thinking, "Linguist, indeed!"

At least this memory was softened somewhat by our fantastic stay there and the wonderful weekend we spent with Robert Ludlum, author of the Jason Bourne *Trilogy*, and John

Patrick, Pulitzer Prize winner for his play *The Teahouse of the August Moon.*

ROBERT LUDLUM, SUNNY, ME, AND JOHN PATRICK

An American couple in Berlin, visiting all the traditional spots, was having a hard time understanding the heavy accent of the guide, when someone sneezed. The lady next to her turned and exclaimed, "Gesundheit!"

"Oh, thank God," said the tourist, "Someone who speaks English!"

Two well-known American brothers with a Latino heritage were visiting on business in Mexico City. Stewart and Morris Udall were raised in a Spanish-speaking family and spoke flawless Spanish as well as perfect American-accented English. Stewart Udall served as Secretary of the Interior, and his brother, Morris, was a congressman from Arizona for thirty years. One day, as they were standing on a street corner conversing rapidly in Spanish with a business acquaintance, they were approached by a couple of American tourists (you could tell by the cameras, the wide-brimmed straw hats, the outrageously colored shorts, and the matching shirts). Without a "Pardon me" or an "Excuse me, sir," the "gentleman" bellowed out in a loud voice, "WHERE—IS—THE—POST—OFFICE!?"

Stewart blinked, took a step back, and replied in the same volume and manner, "IT'S—TWO—BLOCKS—TO—YOUR—RIGHT—AND—ONE—BLOCK—TO—YOUR—LEFT!"

"THANK—YOU!" bellowed the tourist. And, as they walked away, he said to his wife, "You see, Martha, if you talk loudly enough and slowly enough, they understand you!"

In Germany, we find a totally different type of humor. First of all, the German language is terribly unorganized, even though our English language is related to it. For some inexplicable reason, the Germans have never been able to get their direct objects properly placed: "Throw the cow out the window some hay." Or, "Throw the old man down the stairs his hat." And, "He threw his wife out the window a kiss." (*I told my Harvard- educated brother that I wasn't going to give him credit for giving me this, but he needs the recognition.*) Also, the Germans are so precise in all things mathematical that it's indeed a puzzle why their language is structured so.

During our years in the Canaries, we became friends with two German fellows who had built a beautiful sailing catamaran. They did quite well for themselves, taking tourists around the island. One day they had a group of fellow Deutschlanders aboard, and one of them asked one of the partners some questions about the construction of the boat, starting with, "How long is it?"

Now, it is important to keep in mind that these two guys have lived away from their homeland for many years in the beautiful, informal atmosphere for which the Canary Islands are so justly famous. And, his answer reflected the easy living to which they had become accustomed: "Oh, it's about nineteen meters, or so."

The German tourist looked at him very puzzled, and asked, "How wide is it?"

Gerhardt replied, laconically, "Oh, it's five meters, maybe a little more."

The tourist, totally frustrated, blurted out, "You are not German!"

"Of course I'm German!" answered Gerhardt, in his perfectly accented native Bavarian.

"If you were German," sputtered the tourist, "you would have said, 'The boat is nineteen point fifty-three meters in length and five point fifty-eight meters in width! You are *not German!*"

On our plane trip to Madrid, I practiced a phrase I knew we would need when we landed at Madrid- Barajas International to get directions to the domestic airport to catch our plane to Gran Canaria. Over and over, I repeated, *Perdóname, señor, sí usted pueda ser tan amable. ¿Donde está el aeropuerto domestico?* over and over, hundreds of times, until I could repeat it flawlessly. (Freely translated "Pardon me, sir, if you would be so kind. Where is the domestic airport?")

So, just as soon as we had checked to make sure our baggage was transferred correctly, I approached a member of the Guardia Civil, the Spanish equivalent of our police, and rattled off the phrase to him with no problem. He came back at me at ninety miles an hour. I smiled and said, "Muchísimas gracias, Señor." I did not understand one single word, and went to find someone who spoke English!

The Spanish have a delightful saying regarding learning their language" "*El sitio mejor para aprender el Español es en la almohada.*" "The best place to learn Spanish is on the pillow." Enough said!

EXAMPLE OF A CATAMARAN

NOT A CATAMARAN

CHAPTER NINE

GRAN CANARIA, SPAIN

Camels on Lanzarote, Canary Islands

(EXCEPT THIS WAS TAKEN ON THE ISLAND OF LANZAROTE)

There is a very true saying in show business that timing is everything. We had just fired all the musicians in our group for smuggling pot into and out of Canada despite my dire warnings against doing such a stupid thing. They had concealed it in an amplifier in *our* equipment trailer being pulled by *our* beautiful conversion van and driven by one of the band members who we thought we could trust, and then they laughed about it when it went undetected (we were touring in the Mooney—lesson learned: don't be so high and mighty!). We were reeling in this aftermath when there arrived a totally unexpected but very welcome invitation from my famous uncle, John Calvert, to come to Spain and help him build a new yacht.

We were greeted at Las Palmas Airport (then called Gando) by Uncle John, who will be the subject some day of another book. For now, just know that he is recognized as the last of the great master magicians in the world. I recently told another magician that John Calvert is my uncle, and he replied, "Wow, his name is spoken in hushed and reverent tones among magicians." And it is true. This is why I intend to honor him as he deserves with a complete book, not just the few references to him in this booklet of humor. He does figure in quite prominently, however, in the story of our arrival and the first few days in a strange land.

Uncle John had been living in Gran Canaria for a couple of years and was renting a villa from a Texas oilman named Eulan, who made his home there but was in Saudi Arabia for an extended stay. The villa was in the little village of Vecindario, roughly halfway between San Agustín, at the southern tip of the island, and Las Palmas, the capital at the northern tip. Nestled on the eastern coast of the island, it was only about a hundred miles or so from the coast of Western Sahara as the seagull flies. The villa itself was quite luxurious by island standards, walled in, and consisting of some two thousand square feet of living area. Uncle John had built a screened-in aviary on the home's outside wall to house his twenty or so white doves he used in his magic show. They provided a soothing cooing every evening as the dark rapidly swept in from the west and the sun disappeared behind the mountains.

Uncle John is a very generous man. He once gave away a new Lincoln automobile to a young man in India who had been helpful to him. He also gave a new sailboat to a Japanese couple who rescued him in the Sea of Japan. I'll have more about these incidents, and many others, in that later book.

He was, however, and still is, at the age of one hundred and one, an autocrat. "My way or the highway" is the code by which he has lived since he was a young man growing up in New Trenton, Indiana. And when he saw Figaro and Fausto, our two little mutts, at the airport with us, he was less than pleased (I knew his body language well), but he did a good job (for him) of covering it and welcomed us with open arms. We were to stay with him until we were able to find a place of our own as we settled in doing the few galas he had arranged for us in a couple of hotels. (A gala is a short fifteen- or twenty-minute show in Spain, often for tourists.)

On the first Sunday morning, after several days of getting acquainted with the different hotel managers and spending our evenings watching Uncle John perform his act at La Gruta, the most popular night spot in the Canary Islands, we were looking forward to sleeping in for a while. But early the next morning, I was suddenly awakened by a frantic barking by one of our dogs, and I jumped out of bed to quiet him before he woke up the household and the master of the house!

As I raced out the door in my pajama bottoms (I sleep naked from the waste up—try not to imagine it!), my first thought was,

"I had no idea it snowed in the Canaries." The ground around the cage was covered in white, but it was feathers, not snow! The aviary door had been left open, and the barking was Figaro, inside the cage, eyeball-to-eyeball with a mother dove sitting on her nest and refusing to move. And, as far as she was concerned, he could bark until the cows come home, thank you very much!

Fausto, on the other hand, was far more practical. He had quietly and efficiently dispatched one and frightened the rest out of their plumage. I ran back in, whispered frantically to Sunny, and a silent film of us picking up feathers as fast as we could, stuffing them into a plastic shopping bag, hoping and praying that we would finish in time, would have been a laugh a minute. What a scene. All that was lacking was a speeded-up version of Scott Joplin's "Maple Leaf Rag" playing in the background. Even funnier is that we actually got away with it...I think. Sunny says she still believes that Uncle John knew what had happened and showed a remarkable moment of equanimity. After all these years, I'm still too embarrassed to ask him!

Sunny was quick to pick up Spanish and soon passed me, even though I had studied it for four years in high school and college. One day she was in the Supermercado (Super Market—every little grocery in Spain is a super market!), when she suddenly heard loud yelling in English and saw a tall, elderly British tourist shouting at a frightened young girl behind the counter, "RICE! RICE! Do you not understand a simple word like rice?!" Sunny walked up immediately and said, "Please, sir, allow me to help." She turned to the clerk and said, "Este bobo, maleducado quiere arroz. ¿Adonde quisiera ponerlo?" Roughly translated: "This idiot wants rice. Where would you like to put it?" The girl smiled broadly and took him to the rice shelf. The Brit turned to Sunny and said, "My, you do have a way with words. How charming!"

DOESN'T SHE LOOK INNOCENT?

OH, THOSE EYES!

LA GRUTA

OPENING NUMBER

Sunny and I did a show every night, seven nights a week, for over five years at La Gruta, a Sala de Fiesta (literally "Party Room" in Spanish, but the phrase used for "Night Club") in San Agustín, in the Canary Islands. We took over for what was to be a temporary replacement for Uncle John when he had to make a trip to the mainland, but circumstances were such that we stayed, and he concentrated on finishing his new motor yacht.

We probably had many of the one-liners and most of the same comedy routines at the end of the five years as when we started. One might ask, "How could that be?" Well, first of all, we changed tourist audiences every night instead of material. And, the most often any one person saw us was once a year when they returned for vacation from Scandinavia or Europe, in general (or "holiday" if you're from the UK). And they laughed every bit as hard as they did the first time they saw us.

One night, the stage manager, who was in charge of seeing that everything ran smoothly behind the curtain, called in sick. Andy Pandy (Andrés Martinez, the club GM) grabbed a waiter, José, to open the curtain and start the tape for the Flamenco dancers. This was the show opener for the evening and set the pace for everything that followed—a rather important job. José, a very diminutive five feet tall but with more than his share of Spain's greatest national characteristic, *el orgullo* (pride), listened intently to Andrés as he explained, in detail, what he must do. "On my cue, when I say, 'Ladies and Gentlemen, the María Miranda Ballet!', you push the PLAY button on the tape deck, then hit the curtain button to open the curtain. Once more: - PLAY and then Curtain button; PLAY and Curtain button. Do you understand?"

Pulling himself up to his full height and with an air of impatience, José said, "Por supuesto! ¿Soy tonto?" (Of course. Am I a fool?) Just before Andrés stepped through the curtain to emcee, he again turned to José and pointed as he said, "PLAY Play and "Curtain button." José just rolled his eyes.

As Andrés finished his opening: "And now, ladies and gentlemen, the María Miranda Ballet!" José pushed the button, the *FAST-FORWARD* button, and *then* the button for the curtain, which opened to silence and-the dancersstandingwaiting-for-the-music-as-José-frantically-returned-to-the-tape-deck-and-pushed-PLAY-which startedin-the-middle-of-a-musical-phrase-with-the-dancers-fallingallover-themselves-trying-to-pick-up-on-the rightspotonthetape. And José? . . . José was last seen running out the back door of the night club!

MARÍA MIRANDA BALLET
(AFTER THEY FOUND THE RIGHT SPOT ON THE TAPE!)

Henry and Terry, fellow performers at La Gruta, told us a hilarious story of a happening in Tokyo. Their act was performed under black light, but it started in regular lighting. Their costumes were like a black wetsuit, but made of tight-fitting cloth from head to toe. Both costumes were decorated with bones so that they looked like skeletons wearing a black skin with the skeleton on the outside. They did a clever dance routine in the regular lighting, and the cue to go to the black light was a dramatic slowing of the tempo of the music. In Tokyo, they had a full orchestra, not one member of which spoke English. As they rehearsed the show, always in full lighting, never the black, Henry went to great lengths to explain to the conductor as best he could that the tempo had to slow down at the crucial spot, at which time the lights would all go dark except for the black light. The conductor nodded enthusiastically that he understood, and the show went on. At the time for the cue, the conductor turned his back to the stage to make sure the orchestra slowed down at precisely the right time. The lights went out (this had never been done in rehearsal), and, when the conductor turned around to the blacked-out stage and saw the two skeletons, he let out a scream and fell backward, knocking over two music stands and the musicians in the chairs playing their violins. (You had to be there!)

DON VICENTE

One notable exception to the rule of only yearly returns to La Gruta was our dear friend, Don Vicente Suarez. Don

Vicente was an MD (general practitioner) who lived in San Agustín and had one of the greatest and quickest wits of anyone I have ever known. It was hard to catch him off guard. One night he walked into our dressing room, unannounced, as always. I called out, "Hola, vetrinario!" (Hello, veterinarian.) He responded immediately with, "Hola, cliente." (I don't think that needs any translation.)

Don Vicente was our physician, as well as our dearest friend, during the entire seven years we lived there and refused to take any payment from us, whether for services or medicine, which we really rarely needed. But one time in particular stands out in my memory. Sunny had been suffering from migraine headaches from time to time, and Don Vicente insisted I bring her to his office.

After a thorough exam, he gave Sunny some suppositories (a very common prescription for many ailments in Spain) and, as we were leaving, he asked Sunny, with a twinkle in his eye, "Now, you know where to put them, right?" Sunny's face turned red as she answered, "Of course!"

Don Vicente laughed and said, "In the refrigerator, so they don't melt!"

We had a weekly ritual of eating at our favorite restaurant, House Ming, el restaurante Chino in Maspalomas. Tony, the owner, was a very sweet man with a great wife who knew not one word of English and very little Spanish. Her smile was all that she really needed. Tony was the consummate host and always saved a table for us in our favorite corner. As usual, Don Vicente came in shortly after we had received our meal, and we, of course, always welcomed him and asked if he would take some dinner with us. And also, as usual, he would politely decline with, "Ay, no, gracias. Yo acabo de comer!" (I just ate.)

And always, as usual, we would ask Tony for another plate. Sunny would fill it from the bowls on the table and say, "Here, Don Vicente, try this. It's delicious." And, as usual, Don Vicente would devour it as though he hadn't eaten for a week! We loved this ritual!

THE BLOOMQUISTS

We met very few Americans while we were in the Canaries, and, more often than not, when it came to some of them, we preferred not to let anyone know that we knew them. There were some exceptions, of course: the Reverend Carl Bloomquist and his wife, Lorraine, were two of them. They came once a year for their two-week vacation from their home in Rhode Island, where Carl was pastor of a large Lutheran church.

Always within the bounds of propriety, with a great sense of humor, they both were blessed with fine singing voices and joined in with us heartily on our sing-alongs at the Tamarindos Hotel.

I should mention that we played three thirty-minute sets of organ and piano music in the huge, tennis court-sized lounge decorated like a living room with sofas and easy chairs everywhere. The couple's last vacation happened to coincide with our imminent return to the states, and I told Carl that, since we had featured them every evening on our musical program, he was obligated to let me preach a sermon when we came to visit them. They both laughed heartily and readily agreed. Big mistake. Huge!

Just a month later, we neared Warwick, Rhode Island, on a Saturday night, called them, and I told Carl I had my sermon ready. They were shocked but delighted, and we agreed to meet at the church the next morning.

It was a beautiful, old New England structure, ornate but with an air of solemn reverence. The pulpit was raised and on the floor level, but hidden from the congregation was a chair. And so, true to his word, the Reverend Carl Bloomquist sat in the chair below me while I stood in the pulpit to "give just a few words about our meeting and friendship." As I stepped up to the ambo, I made a display of removing my watch, and Carl quickly stage-whispered up to me, "Mel, you won't need your watch!"

I greeted the full house, and the congregation was all smiles with anticipation. "Before I comment on our wonderful times together in the Canary Islands," I began, "I must relate to you the strange dream I had last night, obviously triggered by this event. In my dream, Reverend Bloomquist, Governor Lincoln Chafee and President Ronald Reagan had all tragically met their end in a rush of last-minute Christmas shoppers." The chuckles began. "They were met by a guide—all dressed in a beautiful flowing white robe—who bade them to follow. Making their way down a long, marble hallway with a ceiling seemingly hundreds of feet high, they arrived at a large door. They stopped, and the guide said, 'Governor Chafee, this is your door.' He opened it, and inside was a huge gorilla, frothing at the mouth, eyes flashing, pulling against his chains with anticipation. 'Governor Chafee, intoned the guide, 'you have sinned. You will spend eternity with this gorilla,' and he pushed the governor in and slammed the door.

"On down the hall they went, until they came to a second door. 'President Reagan, this is your door.' He opened it and, inside, was a bucking bronco. 'President Reagan, you have sinned! You will spend eternity trying to break this horse!' He pushed the president in and slammed the door.

"On down the hall, went, by now, a rather concerned Carl Bloomquist." Laughter is mounting from the congregation. "They came to a door, and the guide stopped and said, 'Reverend Carl Bloomquist, this is your door.' He opened it and, inside, lounging serenely on a couch, is Raquel Welch, wearing nothing but a beautiful smile." Hearty laughter ensued while Carl frantically whispered, "Mel, this is a family show!" I continued, "Then, the guide solemnly intoned, 'Raquel Welch, you have sinned . . .'"

Try to imagine the pandemonium in that church! And, laughing as hard as anyone was the Mrs. Reverend Carl Bloomquist!

PILGRIM LUTHERAN CHURCH, WARWICK, RHODE ISLAND

GARY & SHIRLEY

Another American couple that we liked a lot was Gary and Shirley. I don't have a clue what their last names are, but we met them at La Gruta, and they invited us aboard their comfortable schooner that they had sailed to the canaries from the States. One day we had been visiting, recounting stories from home and, on our departure, I asked, just to be polite, if we could bring them anything from town. Gary, to be funny (everybody tries to out-comedy the comedian) replied, "Sure, two hundred pounds of potatoes," and chuckled.

We went immediately to the *Supermercado* and bought two hundred pounds of potatoes (I don't remember how much that was in kilos), and paid to have it delivered right away to the boat basin. We then returned to the basin and parked atop the hill overlooking the slips and watched as Gary came out to the shout from the delivery man who hefted bag after bag of potatoes from the back of this truck. Gary almost fell off the boat laughing as he called down the hatch to Shirley.

Be very careful what you ask for!

SUNNY
PORTRAIT BY SWISS ARTIST, RUDOLF STUSSI

SUNNY AT THE TAMARINDOS PIANO

ME AT MY KEYBOARDS AT TAMARINDOS

SUNNY AT THE TAIL END OF THE TAMARINDOS CONGA LINE

ME GETTING MY POCKET PICKED AT THE HEAD OF THE TAMA-RINDOS CONGA LINE

"GET DOWN, DAD!"
MY DAUGHTER MARA AND I
THE "BIG BAND" COMES TO GRAN CANARIA

MEL'S "BIG" BAND
BUDDY RICH SHOULD BE SO LUCKY!

The Las Canarias story would not be complete without Mel's Big Band. Spain has some of the best musicians in the world, and I decided to put some of them to use in a good old fashioned Big Band, USA Style. The guys got into it quickly, and we were soon doing Dorsey, Miller, Goodman, and more with the best of them. I only had to ask once which number they wished to use for a warm-up. It was always their big favorite: "Tomá el Tren," Duke Ellington's "Take the 'A' Train."

Sunny pitched in enthusiastically, as only she can do, and offered to be our librarian. She set about making files for each of the guys to hold all their music charts and had them ready for the first rehearsal. As she handed them out to the crew, one by one they

112

started chuckling. By the time she finished, they were all laughing uproariously! "OK," said Sunny, "¿Qué pasa, aqui?" ("What's goin' on here?!") I looked at what she had labeled and joined in the laughter.

Sunny had just begun her study of Spanish and had learned, early on, that there were more than a few words that were very similar in Spanish and English. You know, like *mucho* and "much," *café* and coffee, etc., so she assumed that what was inside the musicians' manila folders would be the contents or *contentos*. Very logical, actually. How would anyone possibly know that *contentos* in Spanish means "happy ones" in English? And the reason for the more than usual laughter is that nothing makes most musicians any happier than a little of the weed of the illegal variety. So, they wanted to know: where was theirs?

This brings up a point of which both Sunny and I are very proud. We never indulged in any kind of illegal substances. Never! If we ever found ourselves at a party where it was going around, we left. And that was regardless of the country—overseas or stateside. This is not to brag, but just to sate a fact. We had too much to lose to risk it on some temporary high when our life was already one continuous high after another.

CHAPTER TEN

FAMILY MATTERS

Mara

MARA LYNN CALVERT CAIN—MY FIRST BORN

MARA AND FAMILY, TODAY
TURNED OUT GREAT, DIDN'T SHE! JUST ASK TOM, JONATHAN,
SAM, AND SPENCER!
(RUDY, THEIR DOG, AGREES)

So, should I really have been concerned, experiencing that moment of panic when my beautiful eldest daughter disappeared that day in Vegas? Absolutely not! She worked on the show with us for some time as a dancer and vocalist and more than held her own. We had not been in the

Canaries for all that long when Sunny mentioned that it would be nice to bring all the kids over. We brought Mara over first, since she had just gone through a breakup with her first husband (he was another of those totally immature show-biz types), and she needed a change of scenery. A few months later, after making plans, back and forth, pulling everything together and making reservations for Laurie, Rick, and Lisa (Todd was doing his two-year missionary obligation for his church in Seville), they arrived for some great family times that we had all missed. The kids being together was just what Mara needed and, after being with us for several months, she was ready to face life again. I am so glad she did, since she has three of the greatest boys, Spencer, Sam, and Jonathan, and a wonderful husband, Tom Cain, a former teacher in Mara's high school. (No, he hadn't started teaching there, yet, so knock it off!) Mara graduated from cosmetology school and today owns a very tony beauty shop in one of Minneapolis's toniest suburbs. I never doubted her. I will never forget all of us standing on the ramp and watching her climbing plane on its departure from the Canaries and hearing Lisa softly cheering her on, "Go, Mara, Go!"

Todd

TODD ROBERT CALVERT—MY FIRST-BORN SON

TODD ROBERT CALVERT AND FAMILY

When he was still in high school, Todd came to me and said, "Dad, I'm going to become a Mormon." I thought about that for a few seconds and replied, "But, Todd, you won't be able to drink or smoke!" He took away my only objections with one simple statement, "Dad, I don't do that anyway."

At that stage of my life I didn't spend a whole lot of time pondering the move that has made Todd into the outstanding father, grandfather, teacher, counselor, pillar of the community and businessman that he is today. The differences in our religions have never come between us and never will.

I set him straight by an explanation of my Catholic religion, when I told him the following: "Todd, there is a rumor that has been going around for many years among non-Catholics. They think that we believe 'If you're not Catholic, you're going to Hell!' This simply is not true. Scriptures tell us that our Father's house has many rooms, and we sincerely believe that. Of course, your room may be next to the escalator and the laundry!" (I have to give credit for that bit to the outstanding Catholic convert and humorous speaker, Char Vance. Thanks, Char!)

I could not be any more proud of Todd and his wonderful family! Todd and his wife, Janet, live in Salt Lake City and are the proud procreators of Claire, Michael Todd, Brian, Amy, and Josh. All of them are in various stages of building families, with the exception of Josh who is unmarried and still living at home, since he's only seven years old. Josh is a Little League All Star in baseball (just like his dad) and football (his dad tried out for the high school football team, got hit by a guy who he claims was driving a truck on the football field, and decided he preferred gymnastics and so went on to win a championship meet on the parallel bars, which Sunny and I witnessed, to earn a full scholarship to Brigham Young University, where he finished as a cheerleader for the football team because he separated his shoulder and couldn't gymnasticate anymore). OK, so I like long sentences!

Laurie

LAURIE AND CARMEN THE "ROADRUNNER"

*LAURIE ANN CALVERT BORUFF (CLEAR IN THE BACK WITH A
LITTLE ONE ON HER LAP) AND FAMILY
IF ONLY THEY WOULD SHOW SOME PATRIOTISM!*

Laurie and I, when she was somewhere around six years old, were flying low down Interstate I-495 with the rest of the guys riding with their mom in the car behind. She was riding with me until we parted company, and she and the rest of the family would head on up to Michigan for a family get-together. I had to stay for business reasons, and I was just enjoying a little extra time with this exceptional child. (Actually, they were all exceptional.) As we went past a truck going just a little slower than we were, she looked over at the truck, loaded with hogs on their way to market, and uttered a phrase that has stood through the years and has become a standard for anything that is utterly disgusting: "Oh, ish, they gots pigs in there!" She will never live it down, and could very well become a writer of note on her own.

She has been a great help in editing my work and helping me to make a sentence say what I want it to say, and I hope to see her use her talent for something far more important than simply raisingkids-babysitting-grandkids-holding-togeth-er-the-property-management-company-her-husband-start-ed-several-years-ago-and-keeping-it-running-like-a-clock-while-he-made-a-run-for-the-United-States-Senate-just-this-past-year-which-he-would-have-had-a-very-good-chance-of-winning-had-it-not-been-for-some-intra-par-ty-skullduggery – (I'll let her write about that, as well as the time she was threatened with a knife in the hallway of the Frenchman's Reef Hotel in the Virgin Islands!). Have I said that I like long sentences?

Another time, years later, Laurie and I were flying low down a highway that would soon become an interstate, the Santa Ana Freeway, on our way toward LA, when we noticed that in all three lanes up ahead of us, people were hitting their brakes, swerving, and slowing down. As we got to where we could see, here was a little dog running for its life right down the middle of the freeway, cars passing it with horns blaring unmercifully.

The driver to my left, who was in the center lane, and I each moved to the left, blocking the lanes and tapping our brakes until we had matched the speed of the little dog. We succeeded in bringing the traffic on that busy thoroughfare to a complete stop *without so much as a fender bender*, while Laurie jumped out of the car and coaxed the distraught little beast into her arms and into the car. Carmen lived very comfortably on the Boruff ranch for many long, happy carefree and "carfree" years after that. (Along with Laurie, John, the three boys, and Myrtle the Turtle, who I assume is still living and will more than likely survive us all!)

Rick

ELBERN FREDRICK (RICK) CALVERT II

RICK CALVERT
WITH KELLY, BAILEY, DEVAN AND CARSON

Rick (who was named after his great-grandfather) and I were flying home to the Twin Cities from a trip to Chicago in our Cherokee, when we passed a couple of miles or so to the left of a high ridge atop of which was a TV tower. Rick, who was about ten years old at the time, asked, "Dad, what's that tower there for?" I replied, "Do you see that flashing red light on top of the tower?" "Yes," he replied. "Well, the tower was built to that exact height in order to hold that flashing red light so planes wouldn't run into it." He quickly, and in a rather chiding tone, said, "Dad, that doesn't make any sense!"

To this day, I still don't make sense to him, but I love him dearly! Rick is an accomplished and professional actor and a very clever writer, as well. Did I mention that Rick is very smart? He was and is today, like his sister, Laurie, also fearless, standing up for his beliefs. He has done quite well for himself and has landed several supporting roles in various movies, as well as a great leading role in one. He would be perfect for doing his own stunts in movies. Rick got his start in writing commercials for radio and TV, one of which won him fame and honors for a TV commercial that brought a struggling insurance company from way down in the rankings up into the top almost overnight. He also owns and operates a home-based internet business and is very sharp on computers.

He has always been a clever idea guy. Once, he and Todd rigged up a "ghost" that flew from the top of our house down to the ground on an angle, which made it land very near the path that all the trick-or-treaters used. I am very sure that more than one of them brought home dirty underwear as well as their candy.

We were appearing at the Sundowner Motel in Albuquerque, New Mexico, when we all took a trip to the top of Sandia Peak on the cable car. Despite the fact that I am a pilot and a skydiver, I have a double dose of acrophobia. As long as I am surrounded by a cabin with a propeller and some wings around me, or strapped into a parachute, I am fine, but a short step ladder is just about the max I can take in unprotected altitude. When we reached the top of Sandia and disembarked from the cable car, I was horrified to see that there were no guardrails of any kind to protect us from the sheer drop of hundreds of feet to the canyon floor—almost straight down. Rick walked right up to the edge and, looking down, yelled, "Hey, Dad, come look at the view." My legs were like jelly, and even writing this today, I still feel the terror! He knew full well what my weakness was. And Dangerfield thinks *he* gets no respect! I remember still the tug at my heart when I saw him board the plane, Rick in his Crocodile Dundee hat, bound for home. Today, Rick and his bride, Kelly, are the proud parents of two lovely daughters, Bailey and Devan, and a sharp young son, Carson, any one of whom could follow in his or her dad's footsteps.

Lisa

LISA CAROLINE CALVERT HAEG (AT AGE FOURTEEN)
EVERYBODY'S SWEETHEART

LIKE IT OR NOT, THEY DO GROW UP
AND, IF THEY GROW UP TO BUILD A FAMILY LIKE LISA AND TIM
HAVE, YOU'VE GOTTA LIKE IT!
LEFT TO RIGHT: ANDY, TIM, LISA, KRISTINE AND BRIAN.
WAY TO GO, LISA!

Lisa and her husband, Tim Haeg, still live in Minnesota with their crew, Andrew, the gorgeous Kristine and Brian (another baseball star, by the way), all of whom would make any parent or grandfather proud. Both Kristine and Brian are currently attending the University of Wisconsin-Stout. They cannot help but be successful in whatever they choose to do with the upbringing they have had!

Lisa is a great mom and loves her job driving a school bus to stay busy. Tim is a plumber and, of course, has long hours.

For some unknown reason, Lisa picked up the nickname "Pete" a long time ago. It very well could have come from her maternal grandpa, Robert Gulick, who was wonderful with all his grandkids but seemed to take a special liking to Lisa. Perhaps it's because she was such a pretty little thing, and still is! They, as well as Mara and her family, live not far from their mother, who, in my mind, will always be one of the classiest gals I have ever known!

Mike

MICHAEL RAFAEL CALVERT
(AND A FISH NAMED WANDA)

MICHAEL RAPHAEL CALVERT

Michael came to live with us after an episode that his mother, Sunny, had to go through at a hospital in Washington, DC, while I was slaving over a hot keyboard in College Station, Texas. I so wanted to be there, but my profession has a lot of the same restrictions as the members of the US Navy.

A sailor requested leave to be with his wife because she was about to give birth. His Chief replied, "Sorry, son. You are not required for the launch. You are only required for the laying of the keel!"

Mike was nineteen inches in length and weighed nine pounds, eight ounces upon arrival and didn't stop until just a few years ago when he reached 198 pounds and six feet four inches. At his first checkup at two months, after the nurse measured and weighed him, the doctor came in, looked at the chart, and said, jovially, "I guess you know you have a moose on your hands." I renamed him "Mikey Moose." OK, my brothers are both very close to six feet, my dad was over six feet tall, my uncles (Dad's brothers) are both over six feet, and my mother was five foot two (with eyes of blue). I took after my mother (before she started taking after me for every little thing I did or didn't do, bless her heart!). But my legs, just like Abraham Lincoln's, are plenty long enough to reach the ground. And the streets of our hometown were never uncomfortably close to my rear end!

Mike, just like the rest of the kids, inherited my sense of humor with a good portion thrown in for good measure by his mom. He loved traveling with us, and it was on a trip to my hometown in Ohio that began a series of events that were strange, to say the least.

My best all-time friend, who was mentioned several times in my first book, *How I Quit Smoking and Lived to Tell About It*, Dr. William H. Kuhlmann, was a veterinarian, Hamilton County (Cincinnati) Board of Health president, and gentleman farmer. His only crop was the huge, almost an acre lot of grass requiring a riding mower, on which he gave Mikey, around four years old at the time, a ride. When we returned to North Carolina, Mikey couldn't talk about anything else. One morning, it was a Wednesday, which is important to remember, he tugged on my sleeve as I was sitting at my desk doing some numbers crunching. "Daddy, Daddy," he said, "Bill's tractor's broke." "Oh, I'm sure it's OK," I replied without looking up. "No, it's broke. Bill's tractor's broke!" This went on for the rest of the day and into the next. On Friday, I finally called Bill and asked, "Is there anything wrong with your tractor?" He replied, "Why, yes, it's got a flat tire and a broken fan belt. How did you know?" I said, "Ask Mike," and gave the phone to Mike. Twice Bill asked him how he knew his tractor was broke, and twice Mike replied, "I don't know."

There were a couple of other incidents, one of which bears telling now. (I'll save the other one for another time.) I, taking a page out of Bill's *Farmer's Almanac*, bought a riding mower for the large tract of ground surrounding a home we were renting in the country outside of Hendersonville, North Carolina. I had left Mike in front of a TV watching cartoons, his mom was in town, and I went out to mow the back forty. As I was completing a pass next to the creek that bordered the property some sixty or seventy yards from the house, I heard, over the roar of the tractor and mower, a voice very clearly yelling, "Help!" I momentarily put it off to my imagination but then realized that I hadn't checked on Mikey for a while and thought, to myself, "I'll just finish this row and then go and check him out." Almost instantly I thought, "No, I'll do it now!" I put the gear into high after raising the mower and headed for the front of the house where the garage door was open, giving me the quickest access to the house. As I rounded the corner and pulled into the garage, there was Mike, hanging upside down, strapped into his little pedal car that had been on top of some heavy boxes! He had managed to tip it over so that both bumpers had caught on the boxes, keeping him from falling on his head on the concrete floor. At a distance of almost a hundred yards, through the garage wall and over the roar of the tractor, there is no way I could have heard him…But I did.

A few days later, talking to my brother, the Hollywood producer (really), I told him about the two incidents. Fred does several voices very well and, after listening without comment, he said, in a very convincing Walter Matthau voice, "Tell ya what; if I was you, I'd stay the hell away from that kid!"

Mike, just like all the rest of our bunch, is a delight to be around and, being single, is a definite "babe magnet"!

MIKE AND HIS ONLY ATTACHMENT, ROXY

CHAPTER ELEVEN

LONDON

THE QUEEN'S GUARDS
(NOT, AS ERRONEOUSLY REPORTED, THE HARRISON HIGH
SCHOOL MARCHING BAND!)

It was at Hotel Tamarindos that we met Johnny Douglas, a renowned conductor and composer from the UK who wrote the score to the movie, *The Railway Children*. Johnny also produced scores of albums for RCA under the Living Strings, recorded in London with players from the London Symphony as well as the BBC Symphony Orchestras. He and his wife listened to us for one entire evening as we played and sang, and then Johnny made us an offer we couldn't refuse. He would fly us to London and put us up at his house if we would do an album for him with the BBC Symphony players. Sunny and I wrestled with the proposition for at least three seconds and agreed. The experience was incredible.

While I had made several recordings, Sunny had never been in a recording studio and, as we were making ready to do Scott Joplin's "Maple Leaf Rag," one of the numbers we did every night at Tamarindos and a rather complicated and tricky number on piano, Johnny soothed Sunny by saying, "We have the very latest in technology and, if you hit a clinker, don't worry about it. We can fix it in the booth."

It was about then that we were told we had visitors and were asked if we would like to allow them to watch the session. "Who could possibly know us and know we're recording" went through my mind as I went out to the lobby to see. I was bowled over to see Martin Lee and Sandra Stevens, two of the dynamic group, The Brotherhood of Man, who won the Eurovision Song Contest in 1976 with the song, "Save Your Kisses For Me."

THE BROTHERHOOD OF MAN—MARTIN AND SANDRA ARE ON THE RIGHT

"Of course, you can come in! What a pleasant surprise." I had forgotten that I had told them when they came to see us at Tamarindos, just a couple of weeks prior, about our session.

Then the moment came. Johnny's baton came down, and Sunny went through the piece flawlessly, just as she had done countless times. As the last strains faded away from the control booth, we heard, "That's a take!" and the entire orchestra, along with our guests, gave her a standing ovation. This has to be one of the proudest moments of my life, right up there with watching my kids excel in everything any of them set out to do! Our album, *Here's a Little Sunshine*, was a solid hit in Europe.

HERE'S A LITTLE SUNSHINE

But, you may ask, what's so funny about all that?! Fear not! I'm not through quite yet. The next day, we had a celebration dinner catered by Johnny Douglas' wife, Jan. The food, despite what you may have heard about British cuisine, was extraordinary! Roast beef, Yorkshire pudding, and all the trimmings. When Sunny finally pushed her plate away (as thin as she is, even to this day, she eats like there may never be another meal!) Jan asked, "Sunny, would you like some more?" And Sunny replied, "Oh, no thank you. I'm stuffed!" Now, you Brits already know what happened. In this room full of prim and proper people, you would have thought that Sunny had dropped the f-bomb. And that's precisely what she had done, in proper English society, that is. "Stuffed" is just not said except in the worst part of town. Well, Hail to the Queen and all that! She did win them back by apologizing profusely and reminding them that we're from the 'Colonies,' after all!

Please don't get the idea that the English don't have a sense of humor; quite the contrary. Think: Benny Hill, John Cleese, Monty Python, Eric Idle, Marty Feldman, Billy Connolly (if you can understand him), Dudley Moore, Peter Cook, and on and on. Read on for a couple of examples.

An American was riding on a train on his way up north, when he struck up a conversation with a couple of gentlemen seated across from him. "You know, I just love this part of England." The older man, obviously hard of hearing, said, "What did he say?"

"He said he loves England," shouted the younger man.

"During the war, I was stationed at the airbase not far from here."

"What did he say?"

"He said he was stationed at the airdrome."

"I'll never forget the time that Lady Chichester invited a group of us to a party at the huge mansion outside of town. What great fun. After everyone had left, the old gal took me upstairs, and it was all I could do to hang on!"

"What did he say?"

"He says he knows mother!"

———————————

Several old gentlemen were seated in the plush Gentlemen's Club telling tall tales. One took stage center and said, "Ah, gentlemen, nowhere will you find a more thrilling experience than the hunt of the Royal Bengal Tiger. We'd been in the Saab jungle of India since dawn, when I felt the call of nature. Taking myself off from the group, I was about to relieve myself, when this gigantic head poked through the underbrush and it went, 'ROARRRRERRRRR!' And, gentlemen, I messed my trousers!"

"Well," said another, "we could hardly blame you with a tiger ready to pounce upon you!"

"No, no, no, I don't mean *then*, I mean just now, when I went 'ROARRRRERRRR!"

CHAPTER TWELVE

NEVERFORGOTTEN FRIENDS

ME, JENNY (OF JENNY & JURGEN DUO),
SUNNY, AND LARS OLOF KANNGARD, THE YOUNGER

Relaxing one evening after a strenuous twenty-minute show at La Gruta, there came a knock at our dressing room door. After one of us called out, "*Pase!*" (Come on in, y'all), the door opened, and in came a tall, slim, nineteen-year-old young man with light brown, wavy hair and a very pleasant smile.

"Mr. Calvert, my name is Larsh Shengourd." (That's exactly the way it sounded to us.) "I am from Sweden, and I will go to work for you."

"Oh, you will, will you?! And just what will you do for me?" I asked (I found out that "will" in Swedish is about the same as our word for "want.")

"I will do whatever you will of me in return for you teaching me to be a magican [sic]," he replied.

Thus began a relationship that has continued to this day, with some amazing human interest stories that just keep going on. Over the next few days, we determined that he could sleep on our balcony for no charge, we would feed him, again no charge, and, in return he would help us on Uncle John's boat while I taught him what I knew, which was quite a bit, actually, having observed my uncle for years, about being a "magican." One of the first things I taught him was how to say "magician" instead of "magican."

For most of his stay with us, he carried our equipment cases from gala to gala and would have everything set up for us to go on with the show. It was soon determined, however, that Lars had too much on the ball to be a common laborer in a boatyard, so we made a very good deal with a friend who rented jeeps. Lars used our contacts with the hotels to promote tours into the interior of the island. He contracted for two vehicles per week at the beginning and soon had five or six going. He charged the tourists something like one thousand pesetas each, and with four or five to a vehicle (they were the small Land Rover type), he was soon earning an average of some twenty thousand pesetas, or the equivalent of around two thousand dollars per week gross.

Gran Canaria has often been referred to as a "continent in miniature." It has mountains, deserts, and forests, and the only thing it doesn't have is varying weather. It has a year-round average temperature of seventy-two degrees. * And here's the answer to the puzzle from earlier in this book. Take the first letter of each word, place it in at the end of the word, and it spells the same word backward (I know you are smart, because you kept reading!). * Rain, however, is scarce around the coast, but there is sufficient precipitation in the interior to keep the forests lush. It was about this time that I learned that the Canaries were named for dogs (*Canis* in Latin), not birds.

During one of the trips with Lars, we paused at one of our featured stops: the ruins of an old church atop one of the highest points on the island. One could clearly see the ocean from here, and the atmosphere surrounding the place was one of peace and serenity. There is a fascinating tale about this old church.

Sometime in the late 1300s or early 1400s, a ship of Castilian Spaniards was being lashed by a terrible storm just off the coast of Gran Canaria. The terrified sailors prayed to their Saints that, if they were saved, they would build and dedicate a church to them. Suddenly the wind calmed, and the skies opened to reveal a mountain peak. True to their word, the sailors landed on Gran Canaria and fought off the local inhabitants, the Guanches, and built the church whose ruins we often visited near the peak of Mt. Tejeda. At nearly six thousand feet, Tejeda is the highest point on the island, and the "romanticist" in me wants very much for this story to be true.

RUINS OF LEGENDARY CHURCH ON GRAN CANARIA, DATING FROM THE FIFTEENTH CENTURY

On our very first visit to this beautiful spot, Sunny and I were sitting on the side of a gentle slope, while Lars was nosing around among the ruins. Suddenly we heard the faint tingling of little bells coming from the other side of the small mount where we were resting. A quick but silent sprint to the top revealed a herd of goats being tended by an old woman all clad in widow's black. She was sitting with her back to me, and I didn't want to startle her or the goats, but, before I could say anything, she noticed the goats looking at me and, turning around, her face broke out in a beautiful smile.

She greeted me warmly, "¡Hola! ¿Cómo esta Usted?" I replied, "Muy bien, señora. ¿Y Usted? This simple, Hello, how are you? I'm very well, ma'am, and you? was the beginning of a beautiful friendship between one of the most interesting inhabitants of the island that Sunny, Lars, and I ever knew.

Iain and Jill Carlisle

But before I introduce you to Elena, the Goat Lady, it's important that you meet another couple that will live in our memory forever. Dr. Iain Carlisle, a practicing physician from Bexhill-on-Sea in the southern part of England, was a very learned and intelligent man. He had a tremendous sense of humor, of course. His wife, Jill, was the perfect example of the perfect lady even though she wouldn't hesitate to let out an expletive if it fit the occasion. Nothing filthy, mind you, but apt!

Iain was responsible for getting me into the health system for a physical checkup on a visit to their home. My total bill for radiograms, complete vascular checkup, and interpretation of the films by Britain's leading radiologist, including the pharmacy, or chemist, if you insist, was $1.75 US. I didn't spend one minute waiting past my appointed time in any physician's office or lab. While I can't get excited about our current health system here at home, don't believe everything you have heard about England's.

The reason for the break to introduce you to the Carlisles is that they were with us on this particular tour, and Iain's shyness played a part in our meeting with Elena. As Sunny and Lars approached, she greeted Lars with a handshake and Sunny with a warm *abrazo*. We introduced ourselves (I had, by this time, become much more fluent in Spanish), and she, then, insisted that we come immediately to her house for a cup of tea. And so, we set off following close behind her as she wended her way down a very narrow and steep vale, over hummocks and rocks, around cacti, and beneath stately palm trees. We finally arrived at her home…a cave!

Elena was born on Gran Canaria, but she spoke beautiful and very easy to understand Spanish. Not the Castilian, with its lisp, but the beautifully pronounced, clear Spanish of the

Caribbean. Her father had emigrated to the Canaries from Cuba, and she had been raised to speak "good" Spanish, she was quick to let us know!

Her "home" had the number nine over the entrance, and her son, a forest ranger, lived "next door" (about fifty yards on down the little ravine) in number ten.

Elena set about brewing a pot of tea (she had electricity), all the while looking Iain up and down and not trying to hide her interest as we sat in the very comfortable reception room, a round area of maybe three hundred square feet. This was all of her home we were privileged to see, for the passageway to any rooms farther back was draped with a fine tapestry. The room we were in was clean, whitewashed, and very "homey." She had a well right outside her door, with fig trees and pecan trees in abundance around her property. She also had a big hog in a pen *below* the well.

I never saw Iain so tongue-tied before or after our visit. While she never stepped out of line, Elena made it clear that she thought him to be a very handsome fellow. Jill took it all very calmly but had great fun in reminding him on the way back that he was still a "catch." After a very pleasant hour or so, Elena sent us away with a large bag of pecans and another of figs. We returned often with gifts for her. One that brought a tear to her eye was a large Prosciutto ham.

Wonderful people are everywhere. We only have to look around us!

After paying the rentals on the jeeps, Lars did quite well for himself. He remained with us for about two years with free room and board and was a delight to be around. If you think this arrangement sounds a little one-sided, he more than repaid us some twenty-five years later when he became the founder of a very large financial institution and flew Sunny, our son Michael, and me, along with ninety-eight other people from around the world to his wedding in Bangkok.

ON STAGE AT THE DUSIT THANI HOTEL IN BANGKOK

LARS OLAF KANGAARD, THE ELDER

Lars was one of those youngsters who took everything in stride. I never remember him raising his voice in anger, and he seemed to get along with everyone. We met up in Stockholm when I received a contract to do a solo shot at the swank Hamburger Bors nightclub. Sunny stayed behind in the Canaries and held sway at Tamarindos, so I was on my own again after several years. The people at the club thought it unseemly for a "star" not to have a dinner companion, so they arranged for a young lady, an aspiring actress, to have dinner with me each evening. Lars met up with us one night along with Janne (Yonnie), his little (really little) friend. Janne was a true dwarf, only a little over three and a half feet tall. When he sat on a chair, his feet barely hung over the edge.

As we sat at dinner, the young lady spoke very proper English with a slight British accent and kept us chatting amiably about all sorts of things. Every once in a while, Lars and Janne would exchange some conversation in Swedish, laugh, and then return to English. When it came time for the young lady to depart (it really was only for dinner), they were shocked when she chastised them in perfect Swedish for thinking such improper thoughts about me. Then, with an impish twinkle in her eye, she told me to be very careful of Swedish men! Most of them had only one thing in mind, and they might get me in trouble with my wife. I knew she was Swedish from the git-go, and she and I had cooked this whole thing up before they arrived. It was hilarious! Lars still has his great sense of humor and his ethical philosophy about life!

Charley Norman

This appearance had been arranged by one of Sweden's superstars, Charley Norman, a Fats Domino-type of jazz pianist who, along with his son, Lenny Norman, on bass, and a terrific American jazz drummer named Ronnie Gardner, regularly spent six months per year in Gran Canaria. We became close friends, and Charley wanted to bring both Sunny and me to Sweden, but we thought it best not to take a chance on our losing our gig at Hotel Tamarindos to someone else. While La Gruta was going through some remodeling, everything came together for my special appearance.

One of my characters I had developed over the years was the opera singer, and another was Duart Farquart. Charley wanted them both at Hamburger Bors, which is pronounced

"Hambury Borsh" in Swedish. The entire month was great fun. I learned that Sweden drove on the right, or "correct" side, of the road, finally. For many years they followed England's lead by driving on the left, but did come to their senses belatedly.

Being ever so cautious, however, they decided that they should do it in steps and have the trucks try it out first and keep the cars on the left.

I had the honor of being one of the judges on Swedish TV for a magic contest and saw some very talented young people taking up magic, which is very popular in Europe to this day. Sweden, at that time, was one of the great Socialist countries of the world, which is why Charley and the group ABBA spent six months of the year out of their country. Charley told me the story of how an authoress of children's books was taxed 105 percent on the profits of her book. Until this was corrected by the Swedish tax people, Sweden was the laughing stock of the continent. There was no incentive for anyone to work overtime, since that was subject to a 90 percent tax. Sweden has moved somewhat away some from this philosophy, and people seem to be the better for it.

CHAPTER THIRTEEN

BARCELONA AND SOLOU

I only included this so I could insert the pic of Sunny and me on stage in one of the largest venues in Europe, Las Galas Sala de Fiesta in Solou, a small town just south of Barcelona on Spain's Mediterranean coast. The photo will have to remain small since some of the girls forgot part of their costumes. So, if any of you guys have never seen a girl's belly-button before, go dig out your magnifying glass! Las Galas seated 1,200 and was packed every night of the three months we were there. Nothing much funny happened there, except a lot of those girls forgot part of their costumes on the beach, as well, and it was fun watching the old geezers' glassy eyes! I went every day just to watch the old geezers! I just found it hard to believe that they had never seen a girl's belly button before.

"STUFF" REALLY DOES HAPPEN!

We loved our stay in Europe and, had it not been for the fact that Sunny found herself carrying our child (Mike), we might still be there today. Would we ever go back? Absolutely, just as soon as someone can tell me which guy is a terrorist and which one is my friend! I'll wait!

CHAPTER FOURTEEN

USA USA

"BE IT EVER SO HUMBLE,

THERE'S NO PLACE LIKE HOME"

—JOHN HOWARD PAYNE

"AFTER ALL, WHAT IS HOME WITHOUT MOTHER?
A GOOD PLACE TO BRING GIRLS, THAT'S WHAT!"
—WOODY WOODBURY

Our return to the States in 1984 was fraught with mixed emotions: joy at seeing friends and family we had missed so terribly, sadness at leaving so many new friends we may never see again (except for the Bloomquists), and surprise at the newness of a country that we hardly recognized. What is this "Discotheque" thing? Where are the comedy rooms and clubs that were so numerous? What happened to the big bands and the jazz clubs? We had a whole new scene to digest. Dave Jackson met us with a new Chevy van and matching trailer, and we set off as "Sunny and Mel" to try to recapture the magic we had going before we left. One of the first gigs was at the Ramada Inn in Fayetteville, Arkansas, which had been the scene of so many nights filled with outrageous fun and packed houses. On our opening night, we had only fifteen or twenty of our old fans. How soon they forget!

It did build up over the next few nights, and that weekend, as appreciation for bringing them some business, the GM and his wife threw a big party for us to celebrate our return and to relive some memories from some of our previous engagements at their hotel, such as the time they took us waterskiing several years earlier. To really get a vivid picture of Sunny at her comedic talent best, I will save that story, as well as many more, for her to tell in her own words in a later book.

The Poconos

"The Poconos is a mountainous region located in north-eastern Pennsylvania. They are situated chiefly in Monroe and Pike counties (and parts of Wayne and Carbon counties), and are an upland of the larger Allegheny Plateau. Forming a 2,400 square mile escarpment overlooking the Delaware Valley and Delaware Water Gap to the east, the mountains are bordered on the north by Lake Wallenpaupack, on the west by the Wyoming Valley, and to the south by the Lehigh Valley. The wooded hills and valleys have long been a popular vacation spot."

—From Wikipedia.org (without all the underlined blue thingies)

Yes, and it was in a Holiday Inn in the Poconos where we almost lost Sunny to a new profession. It was during a routine in which she brings some men up to the stage from the audience and proceeds to make fools of them, rolling up their pant legs and tying a scarf around their heads. She then gets them to do a line-dance kick à la the Folies Bergère. The guys always got into it, and the audience loved it. She finishes by giving them each a pat on the cheek and jumping up into the arms of the last one. (One of her very favorite "catchers" of all time during this routine was Sir Sean Connery on the Costa del Sol in Spain.) On this particular occasion, as she was taking her deep bow, the strap behind her neck came loose, dropping the entire top of her outfit. Talk about a wardrobe malfunction. (Good thing she had really long hair at the time!) I still think it was a sign. Somebody trying to tell her something: "You can do greater things than this! You have superb breath control, but your breast control is even better!" She, however, still claims she made an instantaneous decision that striptease was not for her! (Yeah, right! It happened again in Beaumont, Texas!)

...AND AT LA GRUTA, AND IN NORWAY, AND IN SWEDEN, AND IN LONDON, AND IN MIAMI, AND IN FAYETTEVILLE, AND IN KANSAS CITY, AND IN ...

Hoagy Carmichael and Bix Beiderbecke

Inspiration can strike when you least expect it. Here's a great story concerning the events that led up to Hoagy Carmichael penning the opening bars of his greatest hit. After a lot of research, the only verification I can find for the truth of the story comes from Dave Jackson, who agreed that he had heard the exact same story, with the possible exception of the state in which it occurred, from a fellow musician, Jimmy Hakes, one of the guys who witnessed it.

In 1929, Hoagy became friends with a trumpet player of some renown named Bix Beiderbecke. One night, as they were traveling on a band bus on their way home from a gig, the bus was passing through an area, probably in Kansas, that was nothing but wheat fields on both sides of the highway. It was a bright, star-filled night; a gentle breeze was making waves through the wheat fields, and the full moon shone magically on the shimmering, golden grains. Suddenly, Beiderbecke yelled, "Stop the bus!" As the bus came to a halt, he grabbed his horn, jumped through the door, walked out into the wheat field, and from his trumpet came the opening strains of what went on to become one of the most recorded popular songs in musical history. As he played, Hoagy frantically scribbled the notes down on a piece of paper. It wasn't until a few years later that lyrics were added to "Stardust."

"…Though I dream in vain

In my heart it will remain

my stardust melody,

the memory of love's refrain."

—Hoagy Carmichael

MEL & SUNNY HOSTING A BENEFIT

I ACCEPT A MERIT AWARD FROM THE KNIGHTS OF COLUMBUS

Are you a trouble maker? If not, would you like to be? OK, how about just a great way to get someone's pulse beating a litter faster? Next time you have trouble getting the head of some company to come to the phone or to return your call, when the secretary (the gate-keeper) asks, "May I tell him why you're calling?" (this is a stupid question), give a stupid answer, "Absolutely, you go right ahead!"

Sometimes they don't even understand and just put him on the phone. But for those officious biddies who insist on a reason, just say, very pleasantly, "Why yes, I would like to know what his intentions are with my sixteen-year-old daughter!"

Let me know how it works for you. I've never had the guts to try it!

CHAPTER FIFTEEN

AND THEN SOME . . .

The Great Minnesota Svedes and Norvegans

Ole and Sven lived up there near Duluth, in Minnesota and, sitting on Ole's porch on a warm spring day, Ole looks up from his newspaper and asks, "Sven, vot d' hell is baseball?"

"I don't know. You tell me, Ole."

"Vell, it says here dat dey got it down in da Tvin Cities. I tank ve shud go down dere and see vot it is," Ole states matter-of-factly.

So, off they go and, when they arrive in Bloomington and see the stadium, Sven says, "Look at dat big ting, Ole. Dis baseball must be purty big." As they enter they are bowled over by the number of people in the stands. "Fer gooness sakes, look at at da people!"

Soon, they find their seats and a vendor comes down the steps shouting, "Hot dogs! Hot dogs!"

Ole whispers to Sven, "Sven, vot d' hell is a hot dog?"

"I don't know, Ole. Let's get vun and see vot it is."

The napkin-wrapped dogs are passed to them after they have passed their money over to the vendor, and Sven slowly unwraps his. Lifting up the bun, he looks at Ole and, with a startled look on his face, asks, "Ole, vot part of d' dog did you get?"

After living as man and wife for over fifty years, Ole and Lena were celebrating another anniversary, when Ole suddenly has a heart attack and is pronounced dead. Since they didn't believe in embalming, the funeral was held the next day, and a beautiful funeral it was. As the pallbearers were leaving the church, they bumped the casket against a pillar, and a loud groan was heard coming from the casket. They opened it and discovered that Ole was alive! And he lived another five years! But then, at another celebration, it happened again. Ole suffered a heart attack and died. Again the funeral was beautiful and, once more, the pallbearers were leaving with the casket, when Lena called out in a loud voice, "Vatch out fer dat pillar!"

Here's a teaser from the chapter entitled, "Why We Need ERs" in my next book…coming soon!

A husband and wife are at the local mall doing some Christmas shopping, when he suddenly disappears. "Now where can he possibly be when we have so much to do here?" the wife says to herself, very irritated. She punches his number into her cell phone and, when he answers, she jumps on him in a soft but angry voice, "Where are you!?"

"Honey, do you remember the jewelry shop where you saw that beautiful diamond necklace that you liked so much, and I told you I would get for you some day?"

With tears welling up and love in her voice, she answers, "Oh, yes, honey, I do, I do!"

"Well, I'm in the bar next door."

A Parting Word

(No, it isn't "comb!")

I'm sure someone might say, if these are all the memories you have for eighty plus years, you've led a very dull life. Please! If I published *all* my memories, my kids would disown me, my current wife would divorce me, my ex-wife would probably put out a contract on me, and I would need Bill Clinton with his awesome power of defending the indefensible to represent me for what little time I have left. I have, with no small amount of forethought and investigation, put my fate into the absolute supreme court of all courts by embracing the Catholic Church, relating enough of those missing memories to a priest who, after hearing all he could take, gave me instant and total absolution and begged me to find another confessor!

Please don't think for a second that I am not bothered by some of those memories (the look on that little kid's face when I took his popcorn away from him just as we disappeared into the dark theater will simply not go away). They will continue to haunt me, and I can hardly wait for my funeral. (I have picked the hymn I want: "Open My Eyes, Lord.")

Oh, there are a lot more stories that I can conjure up, like the time I was carrying a shepherd's crook through Home Depot (it was to hang a bird feeder), and left a trail of laughter behind me when I asked everyone I met, "Have you seen any sheep running this way?" But I have to take a break. I'll crank out another book later. One, which I keep putting off, is *Disney—A Real Mickey Mouse Company.* This begins with the incredible story of how a lot of people, including Sunny and yours truly, thought we had negotiated a deal to bring Disney to Spain. No, no joke! I will get to it one of these days— before my funeral. Also I just recently got a flash for a great book title: *How to Give Mouth-to-Mouth Resuscitation Without Becoming Emotionally Involved.* I really do need to learn that procedure! (When I learn how, I promise I'll share it with you.)

YOU HAVE BEEN WARNED!

TICK WARNING

Please send this warning to everyone on your e-mail list.
If someone comes to your front door saying they are
checking for ticks due to the
warm weather and asks you to take your clothes off and
dance around with your arms up,
DO NOT DO IT!! THIS IS A SCAM!!
They only want to see you dance naked.
I wish I'd gotten this yesterday... I feel so stupid.

AUTHORS AND ENTERTAINERS ARE SO GULLIBLE!

Aw, C'mon, Will Ya?

The following is an unashamed attempt to get you to buy my book: *How I Quit Smoking and Lived to Tell About It.* If you didn't like this one, you will, more than likely, not like that one a lot more—especially if you are a smoker. Unless, of course, you have finally realized how much it's costing you, even if you haven't yet discovered what it's doing to your health.

Seriously, folks, I wrote the book almost ten years ago and have just revamped it and put it on Kindle for all to see and to learn that it is possible to quit without climbing the walls. My system, called *7 Steps to Life*, that I put together to quit a three-pack-a-day habit, is absolutely guaranteed to allow you to *quit* smoking, not *stop* smoking. (You do that every time you put out a cigarette.) I will show you how to *quit* without turning into Godzilla because of withdrawals. I will show you how to make them go away, magically and naturally. No patches, no nicotine gum, no pills. Before you go spend six hundred dollars (this is the approximate amount of the cost for the two-month treatment using those phony methods), invest the $14.95 with Amazon.com: http://www.

amazon.com/dp/B0094UN554#_and get my guaranteed sys-tem. (Don't you just love the word "invest"?)

IF YOU ARE A KINDLE MEMBER, BORROW IT FOR FREE.
Mel Calvert
www.7stepstolife.com

TH-TH-TH-THAT'S ALL, FOLKS!

(Well, almost!)

FINALLY ...YOU'VE OFTEN HEARD OF IT—AND NOW,YOU'VE SEEN IT:
THE 185-POUND STRAW THAT BROKE THE CAMEL'S BACK!
THE END (REALLY) ... FOR NOW, ANYWAY!

Proof

Made in the USA
Charleston, SC
25 February 2013